Ministry Basics

FOR SPIRIT LED MINISTRY

STEVE EVANS

forerunner
MINISTRIES

forerunner
PUBLISHING
Savannah, Georgia

Ministry Basics: For Spirit Led Ministry
The River of Peace Series; Vol. 4
2015 by Steve Evans
Abridged from *Holy Spirit: Power for Life and Ministry*

Distributed by Forerunner Ministries, Inc.,
　　4625 Sussex Place, Savannah, GA 31405
　　Email: **steve@forerunners4him.org**
　　Website: www.forerunners4him.org

Published by Forerunner Ministries, Inc.
ISBN-13: 978-0692466643
ISBN-10: 0692466649

Cover and interior design by Forerunner Publishing, Savannah, Georgia.

Printed in the United States of America by CreateSpace.

Preparing for Ministry

To make ready for the Lord a people prepared.
Luke 1:17

TABLE OF CONTENTS

Preparing for Ministry

Doing Ministry

Appendix

CHAPTER 1

MINISTRY TO OTHERS

There are two great adventures to this new life in Christ: getting to know our God better and joining Him in the Rescue. We all get to play a part! Of course only Jesus can save people, as we have found out by our own experience. But He delights in gifting us, training us and going out with us to seek and save those who are lost or hurting in any way.

His intention was the perfecting and the full equipping of the saints (His consecrated people), [that they should do] the work of ministering toward building up Christ's body (the church). Ephesians 4:12 AMP

Ministry to others is such great good fun (most of the time) that it can almost become addictive. There are so many outstanding things about it: cultivating the heart of a servant, participating in the camaraderie of good fellowship, discovering and developing your gifts for ministry, learning the art of divine guidance, working side by side with the Holy Spirit, and being uplifted by a wholesome sense of purpose. Best of all are those moments of spontaneous worship, when the work really hits the spot of blessing in someone's life and you both go flying up into praise. What's not to like about it? Well, it's not all peaches and cream, but for now let's take it in faith that you're going to love it so much that a caution is needed right at the starting gate.

7

Before You Even Start

Ministering to others is immensely rewarding and greatly needed, but it is our secondary calling.[1] Unless this is clearly understood, the attempt to be of service will eventually lead to chaos, burn out, or hard feelings. Our primary purpose and our number one assignment is learning how to love the Lord with our whole heart in all our moments and in all our situations. The Lord packed a lot into the "first and greatest" command, but among other things it means that if we put loving and seeking Him first, the other things will fall into place. [2]

> **And he said to him, "You shall love the Lord your God with all your heart and with all your soul and with all your mind. 38 This is the great and first commandment. 39 And a second is like it: You shall love your neighbor as yourself."** Matthew 22:37-39

In practical terms the order of the two great commandments indicates that we have to stay under Jesus' leadership (the first command) while we are trying to be of service to others (the second command). In seeking to be under His leadership, our primary concern is to make sure that we are trusting Jesus with what He allows and following Him in what He asks.[3] If this sounds difficult, then that should show just how much this on-the-job training is necessary.

There is almost a universal tendency to see the needs of the people we are serving as our primary concern, but the Lord always sees the condition of our heart as His primary concern for us:[4] Are we trusting Him or stressing; are we enjoying the peace of His fellowship as we work; and are we letting the Spirit of love lead us? Few workplace bosses would care about the internal state of their workers, only the external results. Our Lord is radically different.

This difference has a lovely dimension to it for it means that results are not what we are being graded on as we seek to serve others. Love is. Our love for Him, and through Him, our love for others: Is it growing? Saint Teresa of Avila wrote that "God doesn't care nearly so much about the work we do as the love with which we do it."[5] What this means is that the wide field of ministry to others is secretly God's great laboratory for cultivating in us listening ears, trusting hearts, willing spirits and loving ways. Knowing this up front gives us enhanced opportunities for cooperating with the lessons.

Now, Where to Begin?

This is the easy part. Pray, then jump right in. Almost always you will find open doors for service and people in leadership who are willing to give you a try, if you are willing to take the lowest place.[6] Starting at the bottom makes great sense. It gives you time to learn the ropes—how things are done in that particular field of ministry. It also leaves you free of heavier responsibilities to learn how to pray as you work. Christian work always needs lots of prayer: for practical help, for heart attitudes, for inspired ideas, for breakthroughs, and for the leadership. Be particularly watchful in prayer over your own heart attitudes. Remember the two "golden rules" of service:

1) Kindness: You can't always help someone the way they want you to, but you can always BE KIND to them. Being kind helps everyone. Few things speak the love of God better than when we show patience and kindness to someone whose attitude doesn't deserve anything but reproach.

2) Respect: You will not always agree with the leadership, but you can always GIVE RESPECT to them. David was respectful of the wicked king Saul who was trying to kill him. Christian leaders won't try to kill you, but they definitely aren't all saints either. Make sure you don't stone them for their clay feet.

The great advantage in getting started with anything available is that the Lord can steer you better, if you have some forward movement going. Having a sense of peace about what you are doing is all that really matters in the beginning. As you go along God will begin to give you clues that will point you towards your future calling and assignment.

Notice what emerges in your heart. Are there aspects to the work that particularly energize or inspire you? Are there certain kinds of people or situations of need that tug on your heart more? The former give you insight into your ministry gift and the latter gives you vision for your field of ministry. In the beginning, while I was still folding tables and putting chairs away for others, I found myself thinking about what I would say if I had the opportunity to teach. I also noticed how much I wanted to help others with their emotional needs. Eventually, I entered into the reality I had been dreaming about.

Meditate on what people say to you, especially if it was unsolicited by you. Those you serve will often thank you in a way that emphasizes the kind of ministry they received from the Lord through you. That's a powerful indication of your ministry gift.[7] Also, leaders may comment on the gifts that they see operating in you, especially when they are talking over what you might want to do next around the church.

As time goes on your sense of calling will deepen, or you will find questions stirring in you about what your purpose is and how to prepare for it. No one can fully teach you these things except the Lord, but fortunately He is with you. And He has had plenty of experience at training new recruits, so carry all of your questions to Him and watch as the answers begin to unfold. In the meantime, let the following chapters help you gain a general understanding of the key issues of calling and purpose, gifting and training. But first a final word of caution.

The Big Hurdle to Clear

Be on guard against offense. Never let it build up. Always go to work on your heart when offense comes and make no mistake about it, offense will come. What's more, it will most likely come in a way you least expect, causing you to feel entirely justified in holding on to it. You would still be wrong. You have an enemy who doesn't want you being of service to the Lord, but he especially doesn't want you to become a *loving* servant. We may have the best of hearts and the best of intentions, but watch out! The only way you and I can become truly loving is by learning how to forgive all manner of injury, mistreatment and wrong—just as Jesus does. That's why every would-be servant of Jesus has to be tried in the fire of offense.

What do you do? Forgive! Forgive until you are holding nothing but a desire for the other person's well-being. Forgive until you get your heart back for them.[8] This will be relatively easy most of the time, but tough as nails sometimes, or you are not (yet) being seriously tested. Call vigorously on the Lord so that you can learn from Him how to release hurt or hard feelings and accept people as they are.[9] Let Jesus be your model and your inspiration for how to respond to offense.[10] This is the growth upwards into Christ that the Father desires to cultivate in you.[11] We can be sure He practiced what He preached:

And whenever you stand praying, forgive, if you have anything against anyone, so that your Father also who is in heaven may forgive you your trespasses." Mark 11:25

As you learn to keep your heart free and clear of offense, you will discover that the Lord will always have something worthwhile for you to do. He only puts us on the shelf if our hearts get hard. That's not going to happen to you, now that you are on guard against it. So pray, look for an open door, and jump right in. The water's fine!

---

1 Matthew 22:39-40: *And a second is like it: You shall love your neighbor as yourself.*

2 Matthew 6:33: *But seek first the kingdom of God and his righteousness, and all these things will be added to you.*

3 John 12:26: *If anyone serves me, he must follow me.*

4 This passage from 1 Samuel gives us insight into the focus of the Lord which is evidently not on the externals which so enthrall us, but on the hidden depths of the heart: 1 Samuel 16:7: *For the Lord sees not as man sees… the Lord looks on the heart.*

5 I kept this quote on my office wall for years, but sadly cannot find it now to give it a proper citation. If you know where I can find it, please email me at info@forerunners4him.org.

6 The Lord is behind those open doors. In the beginning open doors for ministering are usually from Him. As we grow, more discernment may be required, but He seems to like to get us started with many wide open options: Revelation 3:7: *The holy one… who opens and no one will shut, who shuts and no one opens.*

7 Every one of us—from the least to the greatest—receives gifts from God for doing ministry. See Chapters 13-16 for more on God's gifts for life and service.

8 Forgiving "from the heart" is the Lord's own standard for us: Matthew 18:32-35: *So also my heavenly Father will do to every one of you, if you do not forgive your brother from your heart.*

9 The Lord guarantees that His saving help will come to us in any situation in which we call on Him for help: Romans 10:13: *Everyone who calls on the name of the Lord will be saved.*

10 John 13:15-17: *I have given you an example that you also should do just as I have done to you.*

11 Ephesians 4:15-16: *We are to grow up in every way into him who is the head.*

CHAPTER 2

PREPARING FOR MINISTRY

Considering the Lord's high standards, you might think it takes a long time to get ready to do ministry. For some things, yes, a fair amount of training may be required, but for most things all you need is a heart and the willingness to jump into that sea of human need, lostness and misery which surrounds you. Nevertheless, you will be tested on the job concerning these basics, so be sure you know what they are and have them in play.

For you were called to freedom, brothers. Only do not use your freedom as an opportunity for the flesh, but through love serve one another. Galatians 5:13

Ministry Basics: Love

Mastering the basics is crucial for success in any field of endeavor. Whether you want to be a ball player, a musician, or a farmer the most important thing is how well you do it and for that you have to be good at the basics. That's not the way it is with Christian ministry. Naturally, it matters that you learn to do your tasks well, but that is far from being the most important thing. Relationships are the main thing! That's because our number one task is love. Relationships are, therefore, "the basics" we have to master.

And if I have prophetic powers, and understand all mysteries and all knowledge, and if I have all faith, so as to remove mountains, but have not love, I am nothing. If I give away all I have, and if I deliver up my body to be burned, but have not love, I gain nothing.
1 Corinthians 13:2-3

Here are some examples taken from real life: If you fed a hundred hungry people, but treated one of them rudely, you set the work back in everyone's eyes. If you serve the people well enough, but harbor ill will towards a fellow minister you are a stumbling block to the rest of the team. If you are treating everyone with respect and efficiency, but are drifting from the peace of Christ into burnout, you have lost your first Love.

The Lord sets a top priority on love. He wants us to put loving others ahead of any work we are doing for them in His Name.[1] He takes the lead in this for the whole time that we are serving others, He is at work loving and serving us. In fact He is so good at rewarding us that His peace and joy flow in our midst like living water.[2] Nevertheless, if we don't do things His way, those same waters can quickly run dry. Go at Christian ministry pushing your own agenda or trusting in your own abilities and you can easily over-fill with stress. That's not His way. Imagine Jesus feeding the five thousand or healing the multitudes. Does He look worried or anxious? Not at all. The ones who lost their peace are the disciples, a name which means learners. That's us!

Learning how to live in His peace and joy while we serve Him is actually a major key to loving the ones we serve. Think over the many times you have been on the receiving end of someone else's service. If they were impatient, how did that make you feel? If they were in a sour mood, were you happy you walked into their shop? It is so easy to forget this when we are the ones trying to move mountains of difficulty for the sake of the Rescue, but the simple truth is only love *ministers* to others.

Three Primary Relationships

Christian ministry is, therefore, one of the best ways in which to grow a truly loving heart. There are three main relationships that the Lord wants to help us build as we seek to be of service. If we work on these relationships the right way (His way), we will grow in love and He will be able to build the work around us and do His best work through us. These three relationships are the people we serve, our fellow servants and the Lord Himself. The kind of love that is grown and the practical test of that love is different in each area.

I. The People We Serve

Love to cultivate: love as compassion.
The test of love: Are you being kind?

God's love is not primarily a squishy emotion that we feel in our hearts. Thank goodness He does give us feelings of immense affection for others *at times*. When we experience them it is always energizing and delightful, but they do not last. You simply cannot build a lifetime of ministry to people based on feelings that come and go. What we always have with us, however, is the Example of Jesus (who is love in action) and the definition of love He gives us in His Word. Please notice that not one of the following characteristics is a feeling. By God's own definition, you and I do not have to emote at all. He isn't asking us to feel love, but to *do* it!

> **Love is patient and kind; love does not envy or boast; it is not arrogant or rude. It does not insist on its own way; it is not irritable or resentful; it does not rejoice at wrongdoing, but rejoices with the truth. Love bears all things, believes all things, hopes all things, endures all things.** 1 Corinthians 13:4-7

Because love is not primarily a feeling, God can (and does) command us to love.[3] We are to love "our neighbors" and that certainly includes the people we are seeking to serve. Nevertheless, you can breathe a sigh of relief that He does not expect you to feel love when you don't. At those times the best approach is to do what love would want you to do. Heidi Baker, a missionary in Mozambique, asks, "What would love look like in action?" God's love is practical. It is eminently doable.

Now let's turn this definition around. The people we serve won't care what we feel for them (in our better moments), if we are treating them with disrespect or impatience (in their moment). Kindness is our prime directive. You may not feel any love or have what they need, but if you are kind to them *they* will feel the love and be grateful. It remains true, however, that feelings of love bring an inner release of energy, power and delight. It is also true that God has placed His own love inside of us. Wouldn't it be great if we could learn how to tap into the vast reservoir of love and flow in its power? Indeed we can! There are two tried and proven ways of "releasing the Spirit" for loving service.

1) Take out the garbage. Just as clear water will not flow through sludge-filled pipes, so the Holy Spirit requires us to keep our hearts cleansed of judgment and anger, fear and worry, doubt and depression. Otherwise, grace recedes and the joy killers take over. When that happens, negative emotions block love at the starting gate. Forgive, let go, and cast all accumulated cares on Jesus. As you empty out of what doesn't belong in you, the Holy Spirit will fill and lift you once again.

2) Focus on compassion. This is one of the great lessons we receive by watching Jesus doing ministry in the scriptures. Many times what moved His Heart to deeds of love was the compassion which welled up within Him at the sight of human distress. So it is with us. What moved the heart of Jesus will also move our own. Whenever you need to recover fresh strength, look deep into the ocean of suffering in front of you. Get your spiritual eyes off of everything else and refocus on what moved you in the first place: compassion.[4]

II. Our Fellow Servants

Love to cultivate: Love as acceptance.
The test of love: Are you forgiving?

In doing ministry we often have to work side by side with other believers. This is by the Lord's design and it gives us wonderful moments of close fellowship. It also gives us unavoidable opportunities for being rubbed the wrong way! That is also by the Lord's doing. Jesus never causes offense to occur, or desires it to come, but He definitely will make good use of it when it shows up.

The first thing to notice about being offended with fellow workers is that it is harder to forgive them than the people we serve. In the latter's case we are well aware of their need and their struggles. That's why we volunteered to serve them. We don't expect good Christian behavior from them, either because they are lost to begin with, or because their suffering takes precedence. Our feelings of compassion for them are, therefore, much stronger, more readily moving us to forgive them and find excuses for their behavior.

None of this applies to our fellow servants, at least not in the same measure. We naturally hold them to a higher standard—the one we ourselves are trying to live by. Since they are professing to be Christians, we expect them to act like it. We don't want to excuse or forgive them. We want them corrected! We didn't get on the team with them because we felt compassion for them, so we have little compassion to give. To make matters worse, because we are working closely with them, we see their flaws repeatedly. We may even be wounded by their words or wrong ways: "Friction burns" sensitize us against further injury. All of this can make it harder to forgive and accept them as they are.

Now take these problems with fellow workers and compound them, if the ones who offend us are our leaders. They should know better and set a better example. Their weaknesses really do hinder the work. Yet, leaders are notoriously hard to correct from below and seem resistant to both words and prayers. You can sometimes speak with fellow workers and they will adjust their behavior; less frequently the leaders. To top it off, we tend to elevate leaders to pedestals of perfection no one could possibly occupy, and then are doubly dismayed when they fall from the heights. Take heart! All of this is part of the Lord's plan for training you in His ways.[5]

For our love to be *His* love it has to pass through the fires of offense. We simply must learn how to forgive as He does, which is everyone at all times, including flawed fellow workers and failed Christian leaders.[6] He has forgiven you for all that is wrong with you, past and present, hasn't He? He accepts you just as you are, doesn't He? He is willing to use you in ministry, despite your many weaknesses and failings, isn't He? Well, He is dead serious about you giving the same grace to others![7]

It is for our own good. Not only do we want to become great lovers of humanity like our merciful Lord, we also yearn to live in the "joy unspeakable" He makes available.[8] You can't have joy and hold onto unforgiveness at the same time. To be a happy Pharisee is constitutionally impossible! So when offense comes (and it will), drag your heart to the cross (as He did) and do all the forgiving, releasing and accepting there that love requires. You will grow by leaps and bounds.

III. The Lord, Our Master

Love to cultivate: Love as obedience.
The test of love: Are you trusting?

We serve a Leader we can't see. This has unique problems all its own. The One we are meant to follow in life and in ministry is invisible to us. We see Him by faith, but few of us see Him with our own two eyes. If we were walking with Peter and John on those Galilean roads, we would see Jesus turning to the left and immediately realize we have a decision to make: Will I follow Him there? If He sent us to the next village with instructions, everyone including ourselves would know if we obeyed His words: Did you buy the bread? It is not nearly so clear for us in this time and place.

With earthly leaders we can at least look at their expression and know if we are pleasing them or exasperating them. If we can't tell by their looks, they'll let us know. Good leaders give you feedback. They want to cultivate you as a follower. They want to develop your gifts for service. They want to make good use of your time. They try to give you clear directions. Jesus is the best Leader on the planet, but we can neither see Him visibly nor hear Him audibly (most of the time). How does He make up for this?

The short answer is that if you and I really want to know His will in any situation, He has ways of helping us find out.[9] The long answer is that it takes time and trouble to learn how to trust, listen to, and follow a leader who keeps playing Hide and Seek with you! Ok, so why does He do it this way? To grow love in us. Whoa. That's an unexpected answer, but it has to be the right one, since His primary command to us is that we learn to love Him at all times and in all situations. That certainly includes ministry. In fact ministry is a great way to grow a genuine love for Him, because seeking to be His servant requires us to seek His will.

At every point of decision we have a choice: Will I seek His will to do things His way, or will I handle it my way? Love (in God) gives us that choice. Love (in us) takes that choice, turns from Self and seeks to obey Jesus.[10] Our primary relationship in ministry is as a servant to a Master. This is the entry level—He will want to raise us into friendship eventually, but we must first learn to be disciples (followers).[11] We draw close as servants by seeking to follow our Leader in all things. We not only want to do His will, we want to do it His way. This enables Him to work in us and through us whenever we are on track. If we want results, we have to seek Him. If we want to love Him, we must learn to obey Him. He calls obedience love.[12] We have three main ways in which our obedience to Him is enabled and tested.

1) His Word. Do you trust Him enough to obey His Word and live within its boundaries? His Word gives positive general directions and clearly marks out the moral boundaries we are to live within. Serving Him means bringing all of our ways into obedience to His Word.

23

2) His Spirit. Do you trust Him enough to allow His Spirit to lift, lead and guide you? The Lord will give you a sense of the next right thing to be done. That may not fit into your plans, but it does His. The Holy Spirit guides us by His peace. If we take the step He is pointing to there is peace; if we keep love and trust in our hearts there is peace. That's our "go" signal![13]

3) Earthly authorities. Do you trust Him enough to obey the ones He has placed over you?[14] We are not to blindly follow people who are asking something immoral or illegal of us, but most Christian leaders operate within the wide boundaries of the law. Their way of going at things may not be your way, it may not even be God's best way, but we are still meant to give them the best measure of service that we can.

These three great loves—for the people we serve, the people we serve with, and for Jesus Himself—don't grow all by themselves. Or rather, they do grow by an effortless grace when conditions are right, but if we don't cultivate them in adverse circumstances, our harvest will be mostly weeds and rotten fruit! God starts us with a lot of grace, but we have to learn how to work with His love and mercy in order for things to keep growing in the right direction. So, be prepared to refresh your compassion, acceptance and obedience when the manure of unwanted events and difficult people gets added into the mix.

---

[1] Love is our marching order. We are never to break ranks by falling out of love: John 13:34-35: *A new commandment I give to you, that you love one another…*

[2] Matthew 6:3-4: *And your Father who sees in secret will reward you.*

[3] Jesus doesn't hesitate to command us to love at all times and in all situations. There is no time when these two commands don't apply: Mark 12:28-31: *You shall love the Lord your God with all your heart… you shall love your neighbor.*

[4] By the sheer number of times compassion is recorded we should be alerted to what a key motivator it was for the Lord: Matthew 9:36, 14:14, 15:32: Mark 6:34, 8:2, 9:22; Luke 7:13, 10:33; 15:20. Here is one example: Mark 8:1-2: *I have compassion on the crowd…*

[5] 1 Peter 5:6-7: *Humble yourselves, therefore, under the mighty hand of God…*

[6] While it is true that leaders will be judged "with greater strictness" this doesn't mean that the Lord has less mercy, love or forgiveness available to them. In assuring us that He will indeed judge them, He wants us leave that work to Him, not take it on ourselves: James 3:1: *We who teach will be judged with greater strictness.*

[7] Jesus' parable about forgiveness illustrates the seriousness of God on this matter: Matthew 18:32-35: *You wicked servant… should not you have had mercy on your fellow servant, as I had mercy on you?*

[8] 1 Peter 1:8-9 KJV: *Yet believing, ye rejoice with joy unspeakable and full of glory…*

[9] The principle here is that those who truly seek, shall truly find: Matthew 7:7-8 AMP: *For everyone who keeps on asking receives; and he who keeps on seeking finds;* and John 7:17 AMP: *If any man desires to do His will (God's pleasure), he will know...*

[10] Throughout this book I will be capitalizing "Self" to indicate the fallen condition of living unsurrendered to Christ under the rule of our own self-will. This is the supreme "work of the flesh" which places our lives at enmity with God and His will for us. When "self" simply means ourself as the person God created and loves, I have left it in lower case. Galatians 5:18-19: *But if you are led by the Spirit, you are not under the law. Now the works of the flesh are evident.*

[11] John 15:12-15: *No longer do I call you servants… I have called you friends…*

[12] John 14:15: *If you love me, you will keep my commandments.*

[13] Colossians 3:15: *And let the peace of Christ rule in your hearts…*

[14] Hebrews 13:17: *Obey your leaders and submit to them…*

CHAPTER 3

CALLING AND PURPOSE

Because God calls us into relationships of love, we have not one, but two magnificent purposes to discover: 1) the joy of knowing Him intimately and 2) the unique way He designed us to be of loving service to others. These pursuits supply endless fascination! If our life is not characterized by discovery and adventure, we are probably missing the mark on both counts. As we enter more deeply into our purpose, convergence carries us ever closer to destiny.

I press on toward the goal for the prize of the upward call of God in Christ Jesus. Philippians 3:14

Double Duties, Double Delights

There need never be a dull moment walking with Jesus. He has given us two engrossing and fascinating assignments: He calls us to His side to a) know and love Him and b) love and serve others. These two great commands actually describe our calling, our purpose, our assignments and our destiny. We may think of them as duties, but they are also intended to be our delights. Nothing could be more heart-expanding and joy-inducing than to pursue these two great callings.

And he said to him, "You shall love the Lord your God with all your heart and with all your soul and with all your mind. This is the great and first commandment.

And a second is like it: You shall love your neighbor as yourself. On these two commandments depend all the Law and the Prophets." Matthew 22:37-40

These are certainly commands, but they are also promises. If you look far enough into the future you will see by eyes of faith that one Day this will be eternally true for all of us who make it home to heaven. We will become the people who know what it is like to fully and fantastically love God with our whole heart and who love the entire Body of Christ that He is calling into His eternal family. That's our destiny! God has decreed that He will accomplish it for us: we "shall" enter into the perfection of love which heaven fulfills.[1] How much of it will we enter into in this life? That depends upon our willingness to go for broke, betting the farm on Jesus and living for Him, rather than for ourselves alone.[2]

Unquestionably, loving God is our number one assignment—it is the "great and first" command. Since this section is on ministry, our focus here is on the second commandment, loving our neighbor as ourselves. Right away we can see from the Lord's description that one key to actually loving others depends upon how we love ourselves. Many of us don't love for ourselves! Truth be told, we are angry, frustrated, demanding and impatient with ourselves. This cannot help but spill over into the way we treat other people.[3] Once we learn to love ourselves the right way, we no longer need others to meet our emotional needs. This sets us free to love and serve them with no strings attached, just as God does us.

Now we can focus on what it means to love our neighbor. Having a heart full of love for others is a good thing. However, that really won't do our neighbor any practical good. All it takes is one look into the sea of lost, hurting humanity around us to realize that other people need help and lots of it. If we have any love at all, we will want to be part of the Rescue.[4] Some need to be saved by coming to know the Lord; others need physical, emotional and material assistance. Every individual and every people group needs help of some kind.

Called with a Purpose

There's no end to human need! This makes it easy to begin, but how do we find where we can best be of service? We probably all have a sense that God has us here for a reason, a special purpose. Usually this is completely misunderstood. Nothing could be more important to the Lord than that we enter into our high calling of knowing Him—that's our greatest delight and highest purpose.[5] Just the same this isn't what people usually mean when they say "I know God has me here for a reason."[6] They're thinking of some way of being of service to humanity. That's why our first step into our calling and purpose needs to be discovering what our Number One reason for being here is and understanding how to pursue it. Jesus has already warned us that until we get that one in place everything else will be out of order.[7] With that sizable piece in place we are ready to look at the rest of the puzzle.

29

Our calling by God includes a form-fitted way of serving Him in the lives of other people. Some people have a sense of what that is from an early age. They just "know" they want to be doctors, farmers or musicians, etc. and never waver from that goal all their lives. Even unbelievers who don't know the Lord or want to know Him, may have this sense of direction which comes from God. They just won't say it's a calling, because that implies that there is a God who has a claim on them and they don't want to answer His call. But what of us who know that our God is gloriously Alive, can speak for Himself, and has a great plan for our life? Sometimes we can wander in the wilderness for years, never discovering our special purpose. *That seems so unfair!*

Fortunately, there are ways of finding out what our special purpose is. These are tried and proven ways, but none of them are guaranteed to work on their own apart from God. The Lord is sovereign. He has His own ways of dealing with us and He knows only too well how quick we are to wriggle off the hook. What hooks us in terms of service is wanting to know our special calling and gifts. Of course He wants us to know those things too, but He also may be interested in helping us learn how to be guided by Him while He has our attention. Additionally, He may want to check out the true level of our surrender to Him, as in "God I will do anything for you, but…"[8] If you want to walk with the Lord you have to get off your "buts"!

1) Nudges. What tugs at your heart? In your head you may have all kinds of ideas about how humanity needs to be helped.[9] The Lord is far more interested in growing love, so look to your heart. What situations of human need actually move you to tears, or to deep feelings of compassion? Jesus Himself was often moved to specific ministry on the basis of compassion for the human suffering He saw. Therefore, we can expect that God will draw us into our fields of harvest the same way. Learning the way of the heart does not come easily to many Westerners. That's why seeking our calling gives the Lord such excellent teaching opportunities.

2) Drawings. What people group(s) are you drawn to? Paul had a dream in which a man called him to come to Macedonia.[10] God still calls us to people groups, though the ways we hear it are varied. People groups come in all sizes and shapes. Those with an evangelist's calling will constantly be thinking about people who need to be saved. They may narrow it down even more with their concern for unsaved people of a certain region, ethnic group, or age group. Other people will find themselves thinking about how kids in the inner city could be helped, if someone would work with them during after school hours. Or, you may just love talking with the "old folks" and only need to see some practical way to link up your heart attachment with something that looks like service.

3) Gifts. What gifts are you discovering? As we try our hand at various ways of serving people we inevitably discover what we are good at (and not so good at). Let your strengths lead you.[11] Things that come easily to you are a sign of prior giftedness from the Lord. So is affirmation from the people you work with as well as from the ones you serve. Other people will notice and affirm gifts operating in you that you might be totally unaware of. These in turn will point you towards your ultimate main channels of service. This is why it matters less where we start serving, than that we start. Once we get going the Lord can more readily steer us.

4) Listening. Are you learning the way of guidance? We have not just been given a Book to follow, as helpful as that is. Our guide in life is none other than the Lord Himself. Jesus still calls us to follow Him, just as surely and as intimately as the original invitation came to those first disciples in Galilee. Jesus may have dropped out of sight—we don't get to see His steps as they did—but in exchange He has given His Spirit to live within us. Entering into the fullness of our calling, inescapably means entering into the fullness of new life in the Holy Spirit. Learning to be guided by the Holy Spirit is, therefore, essential for the pursuit of our calling.

Convergence

Making all of this come together is the Lord's work. Our part is to be surrendered and committed to Him, to be courageous at following His guidance, and to listen in a searching way to our own heart.[12] Deep is calling to deep.[13] If we keep answering the call, He will lead and draw us through many unforeseeable events which will both grow and guide us. Eventually, God willing, we will emerge from all the training into a season in life where our gift set comes together with our sense of calling. Our destined purpose draws near!

In this season—it's called convergence—work actually becomes play. We end up doing what we have been designed by God to do best and may even get paid for it. Amazing. But be forewarned: One study found that only a very small percentage of pastors could say that they were experiencing convergence. Most felt that they had not entered into the best use of their gifts or had somehow become sidelined along the way. These are the people we expect to have the surest sense of calling![14]

Don't let anything discourage you. You are not them. It all hangs on just how far you want to go in following Jesus. Be determined to go the distance, to the last measure of sacrifice and surrender, and He will lead you into the promised land of convergence and destiny.

---

[1] Paul says that in "all things" God is working towards His ultimate purpose which is our glorification as true "sons" who display all that is in Jesus. We are "called" by God to be as loving as Jesus (among other things) and God Himself will accomplish it: Romans 8:28-30: *He also predestined to be conformed to the image of his Son.*

[2] 2 Corinthians 5:14-15: *That those who live might no longer live for themselves.*

[3] If you need help learning how to love and accept yourself the way God does, then please see "Love Thyself" at www.healingstreamsusa.org.

[4] There are three points to the story of the "Good Samaritan" that we don't want to miss: 1) Jesus told it in answer to a question about the second commandment (just what we are examining here), 2) our "neighbor" is anyone in need, and 3) love is compassion for human

suffering *in action*. Jesus didn't praise the Samaritan because he felt love, but because he *did* love. See Luke 25-37.

[5] Philippians 3:7-8: *The surpassing worth of knowing Christ Jesus my Lord*.

[6] Having worked with addicts and people "on the streets" for over 20 years, I have been shown countless scars and told unnerving tales of escapes from certain death, all ending with "I know God is keeping me alive for a reason." Naturally, I ask what that reason is. *No one* has yet to tell me. They all say they don't know. That's when I take them to these two commands to help them understand what God is up to in their lives. It's great good fun to turn the lights on with God's help. What hangs things up is that initially they always see purpose as service to others, never as truly knowing and loving God.

[7] Putting Jesus first ensures that the other things will fall into place: Matthew 6:33: *Seek first the kingdom of God and his righteousness, and all these things will be added to you*.

[8] As a pastor and former missionary, I have heard these stories told two ways: 1) after years of running from God's call, the wilderness weary soul finally caves in, opens up, surrenders and then hears the Lord say: "But I was never asking you to do that or go there!" *or*, 2) the surrendered one is sent where he/she feared and ends up loving it!

[9] By the way, intellectuals who had a "head" love for humanity in general terms have been the scourge of humanity in practical terms: Lenin, Stalin, Mao Zedong, Pol Pot, Castro, etc. We would have all been better off if they had grown compassion, rather than ideas.

[10] Acts 16:9-10: *And a vision appeared to Paul in the night: a man of Macedonia...*

[11] Weaknesses will always help you work with humility and compassion, if you let them. They are great for drawing us back to the Lord in brokenness and surrender, but they are not gifts for service! Thank God, we are usually called on the basis of what feel like strengths. However, fears are different. Your strength may be teaching, but you are afraid of speaking in public. Do it anyway!

[12] Proverbs 4:23: *Keep your heart with all vigilance, for from it flow the springs of life*.

[13] Psalms 42:7: *Deep calls to deep at the roar of your waterfalls…*

[14] Being a pastor, I know that there are special challenges and temptations which confuse the issue of living for Jesus in the midst of serving the church. "Religious" traditions and spiritual misconceptions abound. It is, after all, a profession that the enemy has been attacking for centuries.

CHAPTER 4

THE SCHOOL OF THE SPIRIT

There are lessons of the Lord which can be described in a classroom, but can only be imparted by the Spirit in the school of daily life. Being trained for ministry includes character development and spiritual growth, so expect on the job training to continue no matter what you are doing. That means leaning to survive trials and eventually thrive in the midst of them. Fortunately for all of us, our Teacher is also our Comforter and Best Friend!

"I am the true vine, and my Father is the vinedresser. Every branch of mine that does not bear fruit he takes away, and every branch that does bear fruit he prunes, that it may bear more fruit." John 15:1-2

Internal Instruction

Without a doubt the Holy Spirit is the best Teacher on earth.[1] Nothing escapes His attention. He is always working to help us do our best and be our best. If you have ever watched the Olympics, then you have probably seen athletes huddle up with their coaches after events. Even if they did spectacularly well, the coach will whisper words to them about how to improve for the next set. Similarly, the Holy Spirit will frequently bring to your mind ways in which you can improve your game as a servant of others. He has a lot to teach us!

Fortunately, the Lord is pleased with any step we take in the right direction and He never reproaches us for missteps, but He loves us too much to let us get the big head. Helping others leaves us open to temptation by pride because, after all, our good works are on public display. Naturally we want to do well—and He desires that for us too—but there is a hidden danger in success: taking credit to ourselves, or thinking that we have arrived at a pinnacle of achievement. So, expect it that your greatest encourager is also your most devoted critic.[2]

Not only is the Lord keenly interested in cultivating our abilities, He also wants to preserve our humility, so that we will remain teachable. If we are open to it, we are now learners for life in the great, never-ending School of the Spirit. This can keep everything that we do fresh and exciting for we who enroll in this course of instruction are always seeking to grow better at loving people and more effective at serving them. It can also open doors (if you let it) for the enemy to harass or oppress you with self-condemning thoughts.[3] Learning to separate out conviction by the Spirit from condemnation by the enemy is part of the on the job training we need.

Nine Lessons

This list is not all-inclusive. It's simply an overview of certain basic lessons that the Lord will likely be working on with you as you work with Him.

36

1) Connection. Just as batteries don't last long without a re-charge, none of us can stay "in the Spirit" and advance the kingdom without staying closely connected to the One who desires to work through us.[4] Jesus has given us five main ways of connecting to Him. Service is one of those ways, but staying refreshed and ready for anything means that we will need to learn how to keep the other four in good working condition: Bible, prayer, worship and fellowship. You will learn, if you are open to the lessons, that no matter how much you have to do for the Lord, the most important thing is staying well-connected to Him. It's our #1 assignment.

2) Criticism. Just because we are stepping out of our complacency or our comfort zones to do something noble for the Lord, doesn't mean critics, naysayers and busybodies will leave us alone. If they bother you, don't waste time trying to change them (or worse, becoming a complainer yourself). You could sooner bail out the ocean than change the sea of humanity around you. Let the barrage of negativity from others (when it happens) turn you away from seeking to please people and re-focus on Jesus and how He sees you. Are you here to please others or God? Criticism can help you see things about yourself you need to work on, even if the only thing that needs changing is your reaction to it.

3) Dependence. Entering into the Lord's work usually means discovering how little we have to bring to the table, like the disciples must have felt when asked by Jesus to feed the multitude. Seen

37

from the outside we almost never seem to have enough: more money is needed for the work, or more resources, or more people. Seen from the inside, we can't help but notice our weaknesses and inadequacies. This is likely an uncomfortable position for many of us in the beginning, but it is teaching the life-long lesson of depending upon the Lord to be our faithful Source and supply.

4) Guidance. We may be perfectly willing to say with Jesus, "Behold, I come to do your will" and yet not have a clue how to place ourselves under His leadership.[5] If we are willing to begin at the lowest level, serving the Lord's will is easy: just place yourself under the leaders He has already placed over the work. Eventually, though, you will start seeing needs that you would like to reach out to directly. This naturally causes us to pray and seek the Lord for guidance. Learn to watch for the opportunities His Hands provide and listen for the ideas He brings you. Guidance is an art best learned on the job, not in the arm chair.

5) Waiting. No one likes waiting these days. There is so much hurry up and impatience all around. Yet, waiting on God is a huge theme in the Bible, especially in the Old Testament.[6] Waiting is akin to hope and is infused with faith that the things we had to commit to the Lord (because they aren't happening now!) will come in due time, if we persevere while we are waiting. Christian ministry teaches us to be patient a) because without patience we will inevitably become unkind and that will never do, and b) so many things have to be prayed for in order for the Lord to bring them about. There's no point in holding your breath or drumming your fingers when what needs doing requires the Spirit's wooing in someone else's life. God's timing cannot be forced, especially since His priority is working on hearts. As you learn to wait, be sure to learn how to "enter into His rest" and "possess your soul" with patience.[7]

6) Weakness.[8] Don't we love leading with our strengths? Don't we wish we didn't have any weaknesses getting in the way? Strengths are a joy. We can get things done with them! Weaknesses are a bother all the way around. Nevertheless, the call of the Lord brings us face to face with our weakness, time and time again. Why? Wouldn't we be better off without them? In fact we would do well to learn to see weaknesses as friends in disguise, not enemies to be feared. Our weaknesses lead us to Christ, reminding us to pray, to cast our hope on Him, and to cling to Him. Strengths usually throw us back into total reliance upon ourselves. Weaknesses teach us the high and holy way of dependence upon the Lord.

7) Busyness. Jesus said He needed to be about His Father's "business."[9] He never said He needed to be busy. Busyness is a modern plague. For those who have caught the bad infection it feels good—most of the time. It really feels like one is making progress at getting things done. But what happened to the peace of Christ? What happened to the leadership of the

Holy Spirit? What about the people who were steam-rolled as you pressed your agenda forward? The one who has learned the ways of the Lord gets more done with less effort, because the Holy Spirit is supplying strength and synchronizing events. Busyness is like an overfilled cup of coffee, sure to scorch someone when it's spilled, most frequently the holder. Let the Lord teach you when enough is enough.[10]

8) Rescuing. There is only room for One Rescuer on the team.[11] That position is already filled! Jesus cares for each individual we are trying to serve infinitely more than we ever will, but He has His own way of working with them and His own timing about it. We can easily get in His way, if we seize things to ourselves, trying to fix people in our own strength.[12] Learn to let your hand rest lightly on your plans and your desires.[13] God often rules by over-ruling us. This is frustrating, but necessary. He knows what He's doing; we don't. At the same time the enemy loves to obstruct and oppose the work. When do we submit to God; when do we resist the devil? This calls for real discernment. Patient perseverance usually wins the day, though the victory may come days later than you originally expected.

9) Submission. We are to "submit to one another" keeping the "unity of the Spirit in the bond of peace."[14] Here is where the rubber of gospel truth meets the hard road of daily life. There are so many bumps in the road when it comes to working with others! Yet, the most important thing about the work is the relationships: with the people being served, with fellow workers and with our leaders in the field. The Holy Spirit is watching carefully over all of this. Of course He hates it when we are mistreated, abused or oppressed, but neither is there any place in Christian ministry for us to adopt an attitude of self-pity, wounded pride, or resentment. Learn to be far less concerned about how you are treated, than how you treat others.[15]

Tests and Trials

There is a difference between tests and trials. Without drawing too fine a distinction, let's just say that tests represent the kinds of situations we face most days. Seeking to be of service will test us in the various ways listed above, among others. Be ready for pop quizzes. Life hands them out all the time! Staying connected to the Lord and talking things over with experienced friends takes care of most things. You will find yourself learning all kinds of lessons through the ordinary cycle of trouble and resolution. These are usually felt as minor disturbances in the flow of work and as fairly normal emotional reactions. Above it all we usually have a sense of passing the tests and growing in faith and grace.

Trials, however, are more difficult and disturbing. We usually have a feeling of being caught in them, of regressing to previous levels of weakness, and of being too piercingly aware of our moral shortcomings. We don't feel like we are passing at all. In fact it is the Lord who "passes" the test of any trial worthy of being called a trial.[16] He proves His strength of heart to us: His faithfulness and His mercy triumph over our dilemma and lead us out. This takes time. If (or when) you get caught in a trial, try to remember that He only disciplines in love. Once you recover your trust and confidence in God—at a new level—the trial has done its work.

Neither tests, nor trials, are a sign of His displeasure. He is genuinely pleased that you are seeking to serve Him. He loves you and He is really, really easy to please. Trials and tests are His "strange" way of working with us to liberate us in areas of our life where words alone could never have accomplished the work.[17] He takes us through experiences that we might have shunned before we decided to follow Him, or overlooked by primarily being focused on ourselves, rather than the needs of others. He is delighted to have us on his team. He wishes to reward us for our service with greater freedom and with a closer walk with Him. Therefore, He disciplines or trains us through tests and trials. It is actually a profound sign of His favor, though a hard one (at times) to interpret.

> **My child, don't reject the Lord's discipline, and don't be upset when he corrects you. For the Lord corrects those he loves, just as a father corrects a child in whom he delights.**
> Proverbs 3:11-12 NLT

---

[1] Holy Spirit's task is to lead us into nothing less than all truth: John 16:12-13: *When the Spirit of truth comes, he will guide you into all the truth...;*

Much of what He has to teach us is beyond our unaided ability to understand: Isaiah 55:9: *For as the heavens are higher than the earth, so are my ways higher than your ways and my thoughts than your thoughts.*

2 In saying the Lord is "our most devoted critic" I am NOT saying that He is critical of us, or faults us, or blames us, or condemns us. Only that He does have a steady and at times disturbing way of pointing out what we are doing wrong.

3 All condemnation comes from the enemy, also known as the "Accuser": Revelation 12:10: *The accuser of our brothers has been thrown down, who accuses them day and night.*

4 John 15:4-5: *Abide in me, and I in you. ...for apart from me you can do nothing.*

5 The writer of Hebrews is quoting Psalm 40:7, but describing Jesus: Hebrews 10:7: *Behold, I have come to do your will, O God...*

6 Just one tantalizing example: Isaiah 40:31: *But they who wait for the Lord shall renew their strength... they shall run and not be weary; they shall walk and not faint.*

7 Hebrews 4:3: *For we who have believed enter that rest;* Luke 21:19 KJV: *In your patience possess ye your souls.*

8 Weaknesses are not sins. Being easily tired is a weakness. Having a debilitating injury is a weakness. God can easily work around these. Even weakness in the face of temptation is not a sin, but giving in to the temptation is sin.

9 Luke 2:49 MKJV: *Do you not know that I must be about my Father's business?*

10 Matthew 11:28-30: *Take my yoke upon you... For my yoke is easy, and my burden is light.*

11 Isaiah 45:22: *Turn to me and be saved... For I am God, and there is no other.*

12 We don't have power to redeem anyone's life, not even our own: Psalm 49:6-9: *Truly no man can ransom another, or give to God the price of his life.*

13 James 4:13-15: *Instead you ought to say, "If the Lord wills, we will live and do this or that."*

14 Ephesians 5:21: *Submitting to one another out of reverence for Christ;* Ephesians 4:1-3: *Bearing with one another in love, eager to maintain the unity of the Spirit in the bond of peace.*

15 Philippians 2:2-5: *Let each of you look not only to his own interests, but also to the interests of others...*

16 Peter calls them "fiery" trials. What makes a trial "fiery" may be the higher level of suffering in it, or the fear it arouses in us that we may lose our salvation (and "burn") because of it—something that will never happen if we persevere through the trial: 1 Peter 4:12: *Beloved, do not be surprised at the fiery trial when it comes upon you to test you...*

[17] It is a "strange" work, because it makes it seem that God is upset with us and because the One who loves us is actually allowing pain to come into our lives—just the opposite of what we would expect: Hebrews 12:11: *For the moment all discipline seems painful rather than pleasant, but later it yields the peaceful fruit of righteousness.*

CHAPTER 5

TALENT, FRUIT AND GIFTS

The Lord gives talents and natural abilities to everyone as a way of getting us started in life. You don't have to be a believer to be a receiver of these—just develop what you notice. As believers, though, it helps to know the limits of these natural abilities in the spiritual life. Wiser still would be to shift our attention towards cultivating those gifts and fruit which are unique to who we now are in Christ as His new creations.

Therefore, if anyone is in Christ, he is a new creation. The old has passed away; behold, the new has come.
2 Corinthians 5:17

A Progression

In general talents are natural abilities given to everyone at birth, fruit are the good things anyone can cultivate, but gifts are the supernatural way God uniquely works in those who are united to Him through faith in Christ. There may be no hard and fast rules here, but there is a general progression that can be noted. Typically, for those who receive genuine faith in Christ at a very early age, these distinctions will be clouded, since natural abilities, fruit and gifts will begin to appear simultaneously. With adult conversion we see a progression more clearly: Natural abilities and most fruit can appear before conversion; some fruit and most gifts can only appear after conversion.

I. Natural Abilities

We now know that we receive a genetic package at conception which contains fabulous gifts of accumulated generational inheritance. Within it are all of our potential talents waiting (so to speak) for us to discover and cultivate. No one needs to be a believer in God to receive these gifts. Through conception God gives lavishly to everyone natural abilities of body, mind, heart and personality.[1] We all have them to varying degrees. We cultivate them to varying degrees.

Some talents need cultivating from a very early age or they can never develop fully.[2] Other abilities may not be discovered (or even needed) until much later in life.[3] No one is left out, though sadly, many natural talents and abilities may never be recognized or cultivated. In terms of development a lot depends upon the individual and the environment. However, both of these factors are under the direct influence of the Lord's grace and providential working. Doubtless, He helps us all discover and cultivate at least some of our innate abilities, even if we have no belief in Him. That too is His gift to us.

With conversion and the indwelling of the Holy Spirit, whole new attitudes arise within us. Even if we previously had been too timid or discouraged to discover our abilities or cultivate our known talents, all this is subject to change. A healthy prayer life and growing confidence in God, should be sufficient to help any believer recognize and cultivate their natural abilities above and beyond what they could have done without the Lord's help. Even so, it is important to realize that these are not yet what the Bible means by gifts. Any good thing a non-believer can do, you can do, too, if you have sufficient desire to cultivate that ability. Spiritual gifts are what only you can do and a non-believer cannot. Talents come to us through natural birth; gifts come to us through spiritual re-birth.

II. Good Fruit

There are three kinds of fruit that the Bible describes: the fruit of good deeds, the fruit of the Spirit and the fruit of Christian ministry. The first two can be cultivated by anyone on earth; only the third one can be cultivated by Christians.

1) The Fruit of Good Deeds. While it is definitely true that our good deeds alone can never be sufficient to save us, it is equally true that the Bible expects us to do good as much as we can, as well as we can and as often as we can.[4] You don't have to be a converted Christian to give to the poor, to work hard and honestly, to love your family or to defend your country. These are good things. We could call them "the fruit of righteousness" if that wouldn't give them too religious a cast.[5] No one needs faith in God to do them. However, just as with natural abilities, good deeds should flourish in the lives of genuine believers, since we can call on the Lord for help in cultivating them.

> Turn away from evil and do good; seek peace and pursue it. Psalms 34:11

2) The Fruit of the Spirit. These are fruit which can grow in our inner state: peace, love, joy, patience, kindness, goodness, faithfulness, gentleness and self-control.[6] All right thinking people everywhere prize these as feelings and praise them as virtues. Christians have a unique access to them through faith and grace, but we do not have exclusive receptivity to them for they are gifts of God to anyone who can receive them. Indeed, little children whose parents may be of any faith or of no faith, universally exhibit these fruit better than many of us who believe. As with natural abilities and good deeds, anyone can recognize, receive and cultivate this to a degree, but as believers we can enter into higher levels of these fruit[7] and learn the way of enhanced cultivation which Jesus desires.

> Abide in me, and I in you. As the branch cannot bear fruit by itself, unless it abides in the vine, neither can you, unless you abide in me. I am the vine; you are the branches. Whoever abides in me and I in him, he it is that bears much fruit, for apart from me you can do nothing. John 15:4-5

3) The Fruit of Christian Ministry. In the widest sense Christian ministry includes anything that any believer might do as a service to others. However, you don't have to be a believer to spend your life in service to others. The New Testament letters generally narrow this category down into those specific things which we do for the sake of making

Jesus known or for advancing His kingdom: such as preaching, praying, teaching, serving in His Name and doing healing, deliverance and miracles. This kind of fruit is a form of service unique to Christians. It grows out of spiritual gifts that the Lord provides believers so that He can work in us and through us by His Spirit.

> **Now there are varieties of gifts, but the same Spirit; and there are varieties of service, but the same Lord; and there are varieties of activities, but it is the same God who empowers them all in everyone.**
> 1 Corinthians 12:4-6

III. Gifts for Ministry

When we are reborn through the gift of faith and the indwelling of the Holy Spirit, the Lord showers fresh abilities and desires upon us. These are called "gifts and callings" and they go together like peas and carrots. Because of what the Lord plans to call us into doing, He gives us desires that inspire us and gifts that equip us for service in that direction. You can also count on it that once you discover any gifts or callings in you, they are there to stay. He doesn't revoke or withdraw them due to neglect, misuse or failed behavior.

> **For the gifts and the calling of God are irrevocable.**
> Romans 11:29

There are three main kinds of spiritual gifts that we can receive, as well as others dropped in for good measure. These are commonly referred to as the five ministry gifts, the eight motivational gifts and the nine manifestation gifts. They will be discussed in the following three chapters. For now let's consider the difference between fruit and gifts, and specific gifts and general callings.

Fruit and Gifts

The good side of God's promise in Romans is that any effort we put into discovering our gifts and callings will always grow us towards our intended destiny: We can build on this as on a foundation that will never be removed. However, we need to build with wisdom. Character and integrity are entirely separate issues— they don't come with any of the gifts. They are fruit of the Spirit (for instance, faithfulness and self-control) that we must cultivate alongside of the gifts, otherwise we risk tarnishing the gifts, spreading confusion in the Body of Christ and giving the work a black eye to outsiders. Maybe someone's been given gifts of healing and evangelism, but if they steal from the offering and cheat on their spouse, that lack of character will bring their work to ruin. Don't let it happen to you!

Another difference between fruit and gifts is that fruit takes time to cultivate. Gifts can drop on you in an instant. The rule for fruit is that of natural cultivation: sow and grow. It takes a considerable amount of time to raise fruit trees to the point of harvesting a bumper crop. That should tell us something. We sow and grow by cultivating the 3 P's: prayer, patience and perseverance. As we die to the old ways of Self, the

Holy Spirit raises us up into the ways of the Lord. That just doesn't happen overnight.

The rule with gifts is different: believe and receive. This calls for the 3 F's: faith, fact and feeling. By faith we trust ourselves to the facts in God's Word; then feelings follow as we receive what we ask or seek. Ask in faith for the gifts that your heart points you towards, believe in the fact of God's promise to gift and equip you, then step out into service and the feeling of being called and equipped will begin to show up. There's more to it than this, but that's enough to get anyone started.

Gifts and General Callings

Let's take it on faith for the moment that you have been given specific gifts and have a specific calling upon your life. Eventually, you will discover what these might be as you see what you like to do and what you do easily and well. Your friends may point some of this out to you, leaders may confirm it, and the Lord may reveal more through your hopes, dreams or encounters with Him. You have a unique purpose to fulfill and you have been exquisitely gifted to go at it. None of this, however, has anything to do with your general callings!

Every Christian knows Jesus by faith and has the Holy Spirit living inside of them. Therefore, every Christian has the potential of serving in any way that the Lord may ask of them from time to time. This has nothing to do with the way we may be best gifted and equipped to operate. It certainly has nothing to do with our comfort zones or personal desires. Just because I may not be "called and gifted" to be an evangelist, doesn't exclude me from the call of God to share my faith in Christ. I may not have any discernible gifts of healing, but I am still called to pray for the sick. You may not be a pastor, but you still will need to know how to comfort, encourage and guide your friends and others the Lord may put in your path.

These general callings of God are in the scriptures and they are directed to all of us. Sure some have champion level gifts, but all of us are soldiers and may be required to step into any role at a moment's notice. This can easily seem intimidating at first (and at times along the way), because it means that God may ask us to step out of our comfort zone and rely on Him to help us fill in when no one better equipped in standing by. The beautiful side of this is that nothing is excluded from us: we can grow in every direction to some degree and we can, therefore, reap the blessing of experiencing that part of the Rescue.

---

[1] James 1:17-18: *Every good gift and every perfect gift is from above...*

[2] Musical abilities and fluency with languages are examples of abilities that flourish best if cultivated early.

[3] Practical wisdom, patience and foresight are examples of abilities that grow later in life for many people, even those who are not Christian.

[4] The critical issue of our separation from God is a deeper issue than what we do; it goes to the depth of who we are as fallen beings: We not only sin, we have a sin nature. While it is true that we can never do sufficient good deeds to counterbalance what is wrong with us (our sins and sinfulness), the Bible never takes the position that we cannot do good deeds. In fact the whole point of instruction in the law and the holiness of

God is to draw out of us (whenever it is possible) better choices and better deeds. Right from the beginning we see the Lord entreating Cain to do good: Genesis 4:6-7: *And if you do not do well, sin is crouching at the door. Its desire is for you, but you must rule over it.*

[5] Righteousness can be used to mean either our standing with God (which is only made righteous through faith in Christ), or our actual deeds which may or may not be righteous depending upon what they are, as well as our motives in doing them. The Reformers called this second category "practical righteousness" and they expected it to be the natural outcome of people who have received the gift of justification, or "positional righteousness" in their standing with God. However, many converts have shown that a person can have positional righteousness and very little practical righteousness to go with it; and many an unbeliever has demonstrated that they can have a good deal of practical righteousness without having positional righteousness at all. Go figure! Perhaps more discipline from the Lord is needed: Hebrews 12:11: *Later it yields the peaceful fruit of righteousness to those who have been trained by it.*

[6] Galatians 5:22 *But the fruit of the Spirit is...*

[7] There are specific kinds or levels of peace and joy which are unique to us through our faith relationship with Jesus, such as the peace of Christ and the joy of our salvation, but peace and joy in general are in some form known to all.

CHAPTER 6

FIVE MINISTRY GIFTS

Everyone benefits directly from these five gifts for they are given by the Father for the express purpose of building up the whole Body of Christ so that we can be fully equipped to play our part in the Rescue. Considering how important they are in God's plan, it should not be too surprising that the enemy has tried to eliminate or decimate them. Several of these ministry gifts have nearly passed out of everyday experience for many in the church. The good news is that they are all staging a comeback!

And he gave the apostles, the prophets, the evangelists, the pastors and teachers, to equip the saints for the work of ministry, for building up the body of Christ, until we all attain to the unity of the faith and of the knowledge of the Son of God, to mature manhood, to the measure of the stature of the fullness of Christ. Ephesians 4:11-13

Centuries of Neglect

Looking at church history through the lens of the above passage from Ephesians, it's fair to say that for centuries, perhaps as many as 18, the primary office of leadership in the church has been that of pastor. Whether Protestant or Catholic, Orthodox or Independent, the pastor, minister, preacher or priest is the focal point for the local congregation's experience of leadership in the church. True enough there may be bishops or superintendents above the local pastor and elders alongside, but where are the other offices? Paul is unambiguous that in the church there are meant to be "apostles, prophets, evangelists and teachers" as well as pastors. What happened?

The legalization and expansion of the early church in the fourth century of the Roman Empire watered down the depth of experience for most Christians from the time of Constantine the Great onwards. As persecution no longer drove the church underground and deeper into Christ, being a Christian became socially acceptable, even preferable.[1] Genuine conversions were no longer the expected norm—they were replaced by infant baptism—and the gifts of the Spirit largely disappeared. At the same time the administrative structure of the church increasingly mirrored that of the Empire with its leaders holding offices of administrative power. This process actually had begun just over a century earlier as bishops won out over the charismatically gifted for leadership over the church.[2]

These developments were probably necessary for establishing stable order within the church—there was so much naiveté and credulity in those days. However, two of the biggest losers during this season of growth and transformation were the baptism in the Holy Spirit and the gifts of the Spirit. Perhaps this was inevitable. It may have been by the Lord's doing that these aspects of His power had to await a time when the church as a whole would be in a better position to handle them. What's clear is that they were never intended to disappear entirely or stay submerged indefinitely. Throughout history the miraculous continued to dazzle here and there like jewels in a river bed. Then, in the last century a stunning resurrection has brought these lost treasures to the surface.

A Century of Renewal

Just as the Catholic Middle Ages proved to be a period of incubation for those ideas which burst forth in the Reformation, so, too, the Pentecostal and Charismatic moments of the twentieth century owed their emergence to the prayer and piety which grew in the intervening centuries of Protestant Orthodoxy. People were hungering for a deeper, more authentic experience of both the passion and power of the Early Church. Where the Protestant Reformation focused on the Person of Jesus and His saving work, the Pentecostal revival turned its sights towards the Person of the Holy Spirit and His supernatural gifts.

This combination was explosive: The Welch Revival and that of Azusa Street quickly brought the baptism in the Spirit and His supernatural workings to millions worldwide. Revivals and outpourings have continued to break forth, as have the baptism in the Spirit and its controversial sign—speaking in tongues. Despite opposition from mainline Christianity, the movement has spread, becoming the fastest growing and third largest branch of Christianity.

In addition there have been revivals led by extraordinarily gifted healers, prophets with Biblical levels of supernatural vision and accuracy, teachers who have gained universal recognition for their gifts, and evangelists who have reached millions even in single events. Miracles of healing and demonic deliverance have become "the children's bread" once again in the life of many churches, especially those in the Third World.[3] Once birthed these gifts and callings have continued to grow in depth of understanding and breadth of expansion. There has been no turning back! In one wave after another it is evident that a Mighty Hand has been restoring gifts to His Son's Bride which were never intended to languish unopened.

The Body of Christ in the twenty first century is, therefore, entering a restored season of all the elements of supernatural giftedness that the Early Church once enjoyed. No doubt many things are still in a process of growth towards full restoration, but the main pieces are on the drawing room table. Now is the time for seeing how they will fit together in preparation for the extensive growth that will very likely come as a result. Sadly, some will miss out, blinded by doctrines that keep them from seeing what the Lord is doing in our day. That needn't be you!

The Fivefold Ministry

The entry point for all of us into this dimension of Christian living is the baptism in the Spirit. With it come praying in tongues and access to at least some of the nine supernatural gifts. The fivefold ministry is there (when it is there) to help all believers cultivate their gifts and find their place in the Body as fellow ministers, but it is especially needed by those who have been baptized in the Holy Spirit. Why? Why isn't the traditional pattern of the pastor/teacher sufficient?

Pastors are usually perfectly able to equip believers to serve on the governing board, to teach in Sunday school, to be ushers, or lead home groups, visit the sick at hospital, or canvass the neighborhood in outreach and evangelism. That's a lot. But you don't have to be baptized in the Spirit or supernaturally gifted to do any of it! And neither does the pastor. In the spiritual life it is practically impossible to lead or cultivate others beyond your own level of experience. In the Biblical pattern all of the fivefold ministers were already baptized in the Spirit and operating in their gifts as part of a team. This positioned them powerfully for equipping others to join in the effort of a supernaturally gifted Body to do the kinds of ministry which only Holy Spirit empowered Christians can do. Look where Paul places the priority in leadership: apostles first, then prophets. Pastors are not even mentioned.[4]

Now you are the body of Christ and individually members of it. And God has appointed in the church first apostles, second prophets, third teachers, then miracles, then gifts of healing, helping, administrating, and various kinds of tongues. 1 Corinthians 12:27-28

Without question, the New Testament apostles were Holy Spirit baptized and equipped for supernatural ministry.[5] So were the prophets. So were many, if not all, of the others in leadership positions, judging by the above list which includes supernatural gifts. Furthermore, the apostles were frequently tasked with rounding up the believers that hadn't yet been baptized in the Holy Spirit and laying hands on them until they were.[6] It would appear that the Early Church was so universally charismatic that those who weren't stood out as exceptions to be further instructed.[7] Just as the members of the Early Church could look with confidence to their leaders, recognizing the gifts of those the Lord had placed over them, so we need to understand these gifts for the sake of our own equipping. Seeing the head will help us find our place in the Body.[8]

1) Apostles. After Jesus' resurrection the twelve disciples He had chosen became the principal apostles and the uncontested leaders of the Early Church.[9] Paul's apostolic position was later recognized by these men, but was contested by others who sought to gain influence over churches he had established. Others were added to the ranks of the apostles, though the number of "false apostles" evidently increased as well.[10] Additionally, the Early Church recognized a distinction between apostles who held universal authority in the church and elders who functioned as local administrators or as advisers to the apostles.[11] We should expect it then that as this office is restored to the church controversy will likely surround it. How to recognize true apostles?

The first apostles knew the Lord personally and well. They had learned directly from Him and had seen Him resurrected in power. Their faith and their knowledge of God was, therefore, both intimate and authoritative for others who wanted to be taught by them. This will be one of the marks. Another is the way they shepherded the growth and missionary spread of the Early Church. They had a genuine vision for the harvest of souls and church planting. A third indicator was their ability to move in supernatural power. Paul said he demonstrated all of the signs of a true apostle.[12] Perhaps, the greatest mark of a true apostle, however, will be the way the other four offices recognize the apostle's God-given authority and submit their ministries to apostolic oversight.

2) Prophets. Prophets abound in both Testaments of the Bible. The unmistakable mark of a true prophet is Holy Spirit given insight and foresight. They are able to see things that others don't or can't. They can foretell future events through dreams or visions they receive from the Lord (foresight). They can also "read" the innermost secrets of a person through whatever unique way the Lord chooses to work through them (insight).[13] In addition to foretelling, prophets were called to "forth tell"—to speak forth the counsel of God's holy standard against sin, calling the people to repentance.

With the New Covenant there is no less emphasis upon holy living, but a much greater emphasis upon the grace of God to accomplish it. Accordingly, there is a marked difference in temperament between the way Old and New Testament prophets present their messages. Whereas OT prophets seemed to thunder at the people from on high, inveighing against them, New Testament prophets encourage and enlighten the people from below as loving servants.[14] Consider the difference in tone between Moses at Sinai or Elijah at Mount Carmel and Jesus, who is the greatest of all prophets, giving the Sermon on the

61

Mount. Give special respect to those prophets who not only have supernatural gifts from the Holy Spirit, but show forth the nature of Jesus in the way they minister to others.

3) Evangelists. Even under the Old Covenant it was expected that Abraham's offspring would carry the "good news" about their God to the outside world.[15] This happened to a limited degree during the Jewish Diaspora as god-fearers were attracted to the Synagogues which sprang up throughout the Mediterranean basin. The Early Church carried this to a whole new level with a brand new message.

Both Stephen, the first martyr, and Philip displayed awesome gifts of evangelism. Soon, practically everyone everywhere was hearing the message.[16] Nowadays, we are all familiar with this gift, especially after the explosion of converts taking place through the ministries of men like Billy Graham and Reinhard Bonnke. Nevertheless, evangelists aren't always on platforms or in the mission field. Look for them in the local church, too.

4) Pastors. Pastors are shepherds of the flock. This is the office most familiar to all of us, so there is little need to delineate it here. It is modeled quite naturally on Jesus as our ultimate Good Shepherd who (in the gospels) cared for and cultivated the faith of lost individuals, the inner circle of devout followers and the wider gatherings of interested, though somewhat less committed believers. Typically, pastors are the head of the local church and as such, everyone needs to submit to their authority, even those who might consider that they have a higher gift and calling.

Being the head pastor, however, doesn't mean that pastoring is their gift, only their position with its common title. Many pastors are gifted as evangelists or teachers with little God-given ability to do actual pastoring. That's not their fault—it may be ours for expecting them to be all things for all people, when the Lord told us in advance that He gives out five different kinds of leadership gifts for equipping us.

5) Teachers. For centuries the academic model dominated this gift. The great Luther was himself a seminary professor, though there was certainly nothing stale or pedantic about his preaching. Nevertheless, with their renewed emphasis upon the Word of God, many Protestant churches sometimes seemed designed to resemble lecture halls with sermons given like a scholarly address. This approach has perhaps had the unfortunate effect of cultivating head knowledge at the expense of practical experience and personal transformation. In the closing decades of the last century a new kind of teacher emerged out of the charismatic movement. These are being recognized across denominational lines for the power of their gift to open the scriptures in such a way that "our hearts burned with us" once again.[17]

You may not find a church with all five of these offices filled. That's not the main thing you need, so don't let it disturb you. The main thing is seeking to be faithful to what Jesus would have you do. Let Him place you where He wills and lead you as He desires. In any healthy church you will certainly find leaders who will gladly help you get started ministering with the gifts they discern in you.

---

[1] Constantine the Great (272-337 AD) was the Roman Emperor who first declared that Christianity would no longer be persecuted and who was himself a believer. His Edict of Milan (313 AD) proclaimed tolerance for Christians throughout the Empire.

[2] This was brought to a head by the controversy surrounding Montanism. The prophets of the movement needed to submit to the instruction of those with more balance and wisdom. Unfortunately, the bishops who opposed them and successfully suppressed the movement were not themselves gifted charismatically. They didn't understand prophecy (as an apostle would have) and hence could not appreciate what the movement represented or be respected by those who had what they were lacking.

[3] It was Jesus who named demonic deliverance a gift suitable for children: Matthew 15:22-26: *It is not right to take the children's bread and throw it to the dogs...*

[4] This is not to disparage pastors. I have been one for years and have tremendous respect for those I know. Theirs is a high and holy calling and immensely difficult. But they are not the leaders of first rank: That place belongs to the (missing) apostles and prophets!

[5] 2 Corinthians 12:12: *The signs of a true apostle... with signs and wonders and mighty works.*

[6] In Acts 19:1-7 we have "disciples" who "believed" in Jesus, yet lacked the Holy Spirit baptism and supernatural gifts which accompany it. Paul wouldn't leave it at that and neither should we: *And when Paul had laid his hands on them, the Holy Spirit came on them, and they began speaking in tongues and prophesying.*

[7] Acts 18:24-26 is a picture of a Christian teacher (Apollos) being further instructed in the baptism of the Holy Spirit, since he only knew the "baptism of John" which is of water and points towards faith in Christ, not the empowerment of the Spirit: *He spoke and taught accurately the things concerning Jesus, though he knew only the baptism of John.*

[8] Jesus is the ultimate and actual "head of the Church," but He obviously confers "headship" to leaders in the church.

[9] So important was the concept of the chosen twelve that Judas was quickly replaced (after his betrayal and death) by Matthias: Acts 1:24-26

[10] 2 Corinthians 11:13: *False apostles... disguising themselves as apostles of Christ.*

[11] Acts 15:6: *The apostles and the elders were gathered... to consider this matter.*

[12] 2 Corinthians 12:12 AMP: *The signs that indicate a [genuine] apostle were performed among you fully... in miracles and wonders and mighty works.*

[13] 1 Corinthians 14:24-25: *If all prophesy... the secrets of his heart are disclosed.*

[14] See Hebrews 12: 18-24 for a striking image of this difference.

[15] Nahum 1:15: *Behold... the feet of him who brings good news...*

[16] Colossians 1:5-7: *The gospel... has come to you, as indeed in the whole world...*

[17] On the road to Emmaus Easter morning two unsuspecting disciples discovered that Jesus had been in the midst: Luke 24:32: *They said to each other, "Did not our hearts burn within us while he talked to us on the road, while he opened to us the Scriptures?"*

CHAPTER 7

SEVEN MOTIVATIONAL GIFTS

These should be of particular interest to everyone, since each of us has been given at least one. Oddly enough, it's not always obvious to us what our unique gift is. Perhaps the Lord enjoys playing Hide and Seek more than we might imagine. Here's a clue: Usually you will find them hidden in plain sight, since people often live out of their gift before they catch on to what it is. Intrigued? See if you can spot your own.

Having gifts that differ according to the grace given to us, let us use them: if prophecy, in proportion to our faith; if service, in our serving; the one who teaches, in his teaching; the one who exhorts, in his exhortation; the one who contributes, in generosity; the one who leads, with zeal; the one who does acts of mercy, with cheerfulness.
Romans 12:6-8

Supernaturally Natural

These seven gifts are called motivational gifts because they provide the inner focus that inspires us to get into the game of serving humanity in our own particular way. We have an inner drive or motivation that makes us notice certain areas of need in the church or the world and then keeps us looking for ways of meeting that need. All of this happens to match our gift so "naturally" that we may never stop to question or examine it. We might wonder, "Why doesn't everyone feel this way?" and be genuinely surprised that they don't.

Having one of these gifts doesn't mean that we are going to be great at it automatically. They have to be cultivated like anything else in life. And they won't work very well if we aren't in balance with the Lord (more on that later). Nevertheless, the sense of inner compelling is so consistent and so intimately tied into our own desires that it practically guarantees that we will develop real skills to go along with the gift. If we don't, it won't be for lack of effort, since the gift keeps pointing us at the same target over and over again. This inner motivation is nothing less than God at work within us "for his good pleasure."[1]

> **Therefore, my beloved, as you have always obeyed, so now, not only as in my presence but much more in my absence, work out your own salvation with fear and trembling, for it is God who works in you, both to will and to work for his good pleasure.** Philippians 2:12-13

This means that there will be joy in it, because God is working in us to make us willing (desirous) of doing what He is also enabling us to do. It "pleases" the Lord to work through us and He is very good about passing His feelings on to us. This doesn't mean that we can't ever burn out the inner flame. We can. It feels so good operating out of our gift that exhausting ourselves is a danger that has to be guarded against. However, the Lord always stands ready to renew and refresh us. If we allow Him to do that—wonder of wonders—the former desires have a way of springing right back to life! This inner drive comes from His holy fire to burn brightly within us in this particular way and that flame can never be quenched.

For God's gifts and His call are irrevocable. [He never withdraws them when once they are given, and He does not change His mind about those to whom He gives His grace or to whom He sends His call.] Romans 11:29 AMP

Primary and Secondary

As you look over the list you may notice right away the gift that is your primary motivation. If you can't spot it, others who know you well probably can. The Holy Spirit has been cultivating these inner motivations in us since childhood in terms of general orientation.[2] Conversion and the entrance of the Holy Spirit within us may bring new aspects and abilities out to the forefront, as well as unveil for us new applications within the Christian community. For instance someone gifted as a teacher may have been growing happily in that area all their life, but conversion will likely bring whole new levels of purpose and initiate a brand new desire to teach spiritual truths.

Some confusion may arise over just how many gifts you have. Paul gives us little to go on beyond the mere recounting of the list. There is nothing here to limit these to one per person. You could conceivably have several primary gifts and rotate though times of being more focused on one rather than the other. Nevertheless, the common pattern is for a person to have a single primary gift with one or more secondary gifts that complement and enhance its operation. In this way the Lord provides a natural sense of cohesion and wholeness to our inner focus and motivation: We aren't as likely to be pulled in three directions at once! Even so, all of us can (and probably should) cultivate each of these gifts to some degree.

Flesh Verses Spirit

Since these gifts are the Holy Spirit working within us, we might suppose that our gift(s) will always work for good in our life and for the good of those we seek to serve. Not so! It is too much to be hoped that these inner workings of the Lord cannot be subverted by the enemy. Spiritual darkness loves to turn even good things against us. As mentioned earlier, if we don't stay in balance these gifts of His won't operate properly. The key to staying balanced is living with Jesus at the center and with ourselves surrendered and submitted to His leadership. He hasn't given us gifts and callings so that we can go charging off on our own!

As with anything in this new life in Christ, our actual trust in the Lord determines practically everything else. If you want to serve Him and others, if you want your gift(s) to be operating at peak performance, then you will want to learn to guard your heart so that the peace of Christ rules within you.[3] There is no clearer indication that we are yielded to His leadership than the peace He gives us when we are trusting Him and doing things His way.[4] With that peace in place the motivational gifts positively hum! It is truly amazing, even breathtaking to be flowing in these gifts. This is part of what it means to be led by the Spirit.[5]

We can, however, fall back into being oppressed by the flesh.[6] It is easy and "natural" to fall out of the Spirit and into the flesh, even when we are trying to serve the Lord. Because the flesh is our fallen nature, falling into it almost feels normal. The absence of the peace of Christ should alert us that something has gone wrong. That wrongness will inevitably show up by distorting the gifts we cherish and enjoy, turning service into something onerous, rather than delightful. In the following brief descriptions note how being in "the flesh" can distort the gift. Note also the wonderful purpose the gift can serve when we are in the Spirit.

For we are his workmanship, created in Christ Jesus for good works, which God prepared beforehand, that we should walk in them. Ephesians 2:10

Seven Motivational Gifts

Because it is possible for believers to receive the indwelling Spirit, but never seek or receive the baptism in the Spirit, there will be differences in the way these gifts operate in those who are not Holy Spirit baptized. Remember, the Early Church that Paul shepherded was almost entirely composed of people who had received the baptism in the Spirit. Hence, he would have had in his mind the way these gifts look in the lives of people who know Jesus by faith and are also anointed with the Spirit's power.

71

1) Prophesying: "If prophecy, in proportion to our faith." People with this gift usually know it and are eager to cultivate it, because it often brings enhanced opportunities to experience the supernatural working of the Holy Spirit. Prophets have a burning heart for receiving specific words or visions from God which will bring clarity to individuals or churches. Clarity comes by calling people to repentance, pointing out their sin; or through sharing visions, restoring lost spiritual sight. If those with the gift of prophecy have not yet received the baptism in the Spirit, their emphasis will be more on the Word of God, than specific words *from* God. If in the flesh, people with this gift may lose the New Testament tone of grace, becoming hard and judgmental, ministering the law's condemnation, rather than the gospel's love and mercy.

2) Serving: "If service, in our serving." The Amplified Bible calls this "practical service." That's the proper note. The person with this gift is always noticing things of a practical nature that will help an individual or the church, and then throwing themselves into the fray to get the job done. It's been said that love is an active verb; certainly these are the ones who put feet to their prayers. That is if they haven't slipped into the flesh. The danger here is leaping, before praying, and thereby taking the lead away from the Lord. This can lead to misguided efforts, feeling unappreciated or burn out, if left to the flesh. Pastors always appreciate the gift of service (not necessarily that of prophesy!) and they can and should help these good hearted workers learn the ways of wisdom. If this is your gift, try to remember that seeing a need isn't always a call of God for personal action; it may be a call to prayer instead.

3) Teaching: "The one who teaches, in his teaching." A teacher's focus is different than a prophet's in that their concern is more for the whole counsel of the Word of God with a willingness to leave the individual's response to conscience. Prophets are more inclined to "zero in" on specifics and seek to close the deal. In our day a great line is drawn between preaching and teaching, but not in the Bible. Jesus' "preaching" was called teaching and so was that of the apostles—it's one of the main things they were known for.[7] Teachers in the flesh fall prey to focusing on getting the head knowledge right, filling minds with information, while leaving hearts empty and thirsting.

4) Exhorting: "The one who exhorts, in his exhortation." Exhortation is better known to us as encouragement, a word which means to give courage to the hearts of others. Exhorters are always looking for opportunities to do that. Who is cast down? Who needs building up? How can their spirits be lifted higher? Where a teacher wants to help you learn truths you don't know yet, an exhorter wants to help you believe what you already know. Notice how this plays out with different preaching styles: some preachers are teachers at heart; others are exhorters. Meanwhile, some of the best exhorters don't have a public ministry. They just naturally lift the mood of individuals wherever they go. Watch out for one in the flesh, however, if you don't want to find out firsthand what the "gift of discouragement" looks like in operation.

5) Giving: "The one who contributes, in generosity." The Lord evidently calls some people to gather wealth, so that through them, He can bless others and the church. It's a tough job, but someone has to do it. The thing about these folks is their absence of greed and the evident delight they have in giving money or material help away. They usually seem consciously aware that their calling is to be a channel of blessing and they genuinely want to keep the river flowing. If they fall into the flesh, all bets are off: they may amass wealth for themselves alone, or seek a show of recognition for what they do give away.

6) Leading: "The one who leads, with zeal." The gift of administration includes the ability to supervise others, cast vision, assemble a team and chart a course all with unflagging "zeal" or diligence. If this is your gift, then know that the rest of us are grateful you have it! We need your energetic devotion to duty or things would really fall apart. We thank God for your integrity and willingness to sacrifice ordinary pleasures for the sake of the cause. Just please don't "lord" it over us, bossing us around! Jesus said that our leaders would be servants to us and those with this gift truly are—whenever they are in the Spirit. Otherwise…

7) Caring: "The one who does acts of mercy, with cheerfulness." Last, but not least, is the heart of the Body of Christ. People blessed with a mercy gift have hearts as big and warm as your mama's stove. They notice the hurting people among us and launch into prayer, then press in to draw them out. They care less about how you got into trouble, than how to get you out. Unlike teachers and prophets, they don't want to know if you are learning from the experience; they want you free of the pain. These are people you can trust with your heart. Unfortunately, when in the flesh, their own heart can take them down, if they don't learn how to cast every care and all that pain on the Lord.

Put it all together and you have a vision for the Body of Christ as a mighty warrior, able to tend its own wounds and refresh its own vision when all the parts are working together as designed. Discover your gift, learn how to walk in the Spirit with it, and find your place in the Body!

---

[1] Notice that God is at work in us to "will" and "to do." He is giving us the desires and providing us with abilities in carrying them out: Philippians 2:12-13: *For it is God who works in you, both to will and to work for his good pleasure.*

[2] The Holy Spirit has been "with us" since conception. He has always been our Teacher and life coach whether we knew it or not. It's just that until conversion, He had to stay on the outside and couldn't teach us the things of the Lord, or of the spiritual life as He now does *within* us: John 14:16-17: *You know him, for he dwells with you and will be in you.*

[3] Colossians 3:15: *And let the peace of Christ rule in your hearts.*

[4] Proverbs 3:5-6: *Trust in the Lord with all your heart... and he will make straight your paths.*

[5] Romans 8:12-14: Notice that we have to put aside the flesh in order to be led by the Spirit: *But if by the Spirit you put to death the deeds of the body, you will live.*

[6] Galatians 5:16-17: This is the spiritual "tug of war" which goes on in every Christian's life: *The desires of the flesh are against the Spirit, and... the Spirit are against the flesh.*

[7] Acts 2:42-43: *And they devoted themselves to the apostles' teaching...*

CHAPTER 8

NINE GIFTS OF POWER

Jesus never intended for His church to be powerless or penniless. Just as the tithe is the Lord's provision for material supply, so the baptism in the Spirit is His provision for supernatural supply. Neither is forced on anyone, but when believers come into obedience, watch out—the windows of heaven open wide![1] *Through the baptism in the Spirit, Jesus pours out gifts that will manifest as signs and wonders for the sake of ministry to someone He wants to bless.*

To each is given the manifestation of the Spirit for the common good. 1 Corinthians 12:7

A Context for Understanding

The main passage concerning the nine gifts of supernatural power is Paul's account in 1 Corinthians 12:1-12 where they are set within a wider context. Since he was writing to a church that was experiencing these gifts and was already familiar with how they worked, Paul doesn't take time to describe them.[2] That's a pity for us, because many of us grew up in churches devoid of these supernatural operations.

Experience is the best teacher when it is available; absence of experience gives false ideas plenty of room to grow. Nevertheless, we can surmise what these gifts would have looked like then, by their appearances in other passages of scripture and by the way they are breaking forth in Charismatic and Pentecostal churches where the baptism of the Spirit is flourishing today. Before we examine the individual gifts, let's look at the context Paul gave them.

> **Now concerning spiritual gifts, brothers, I do not want you to be uninformed.** 1 Corinthians 12:1

According to St. Paul, the very first thing that we need to know concerning spiritual gifts is to avoid being "uninformed." Learning about something is usually the first step towards doing it, but it is also a necessary step towards allowing others to do a thing. Why does that matter? In western churches many people have pulled away from the supernatural operations of the Holy Spirit due to fear and false teaching. By being uninformed of the truth, they not only aren't seeking to make themselves available for God to work through them, they are actively hindering others from going forward.

> **Now there are varieties of gifts, but the same Spirit; and there are varieties of service, but the same Lord; and there are varieties of activities, but it is the same God who empowers them all in everyone. To each is given the manifestation of the Spirit for the common good.**
> 1 Corinthians 12:4-7

The whole of the Trinity is involved in the operation of these gifts: the Holy Spirit who works through the gift we are given, the Lord Jesus whose church is being served by the gift, and God the Father who oversees it all for the sake of everyone involved. Elsewhere Paul will describe other gifts and their place in the Body of

Christial.[3] Here his concern is only for certain gifts he now calls "manifestations of the Spirit." Whatever is "manifest" has been brought to the light. It is something obvious and evident. These are gifts which make it obvious that God is at work through them! They display supernatural power in a way that the other gifts do not.

> **All these are empowered by one and the same Spirit, who apportions to each one individually as he wills. For just as the body is one and has many members, and all the members of the body, though many, are one body, so it is with Christ.** 1 Corinthians 12:1-12

Because these gifts are manifestations of the Spirit, it is God alone who "apportions"—who chooses who, when and where. Although these "activities" can be counterfeited by the enemy, the operation of the true gifts is entirely under the Holy Spirit's control. They can't be worked up by human effort. This is an important point for discerning how these gifts differ from normal human abilities. For instance, anyone who teaches can convey intellectual knowledge about a subject, but that is not what is meant by the "word of knowledge." We look to doctors for healing, but their gifts are not "gifts of healings." Certainly, God may work through doctors and teachers (let's hope He does!), but His work is hidden, not manifest, except in outcome. These nine gifts manifest *during* the process of ministering to others.

The Nine Gifts of Power

For to one is given the word of wisdom through the Spirit, to another the word of knowledge through the same Spirit, to another faith by the same Spirit, to another gifts of healings by the same Spirit, to another the working of miracles, to another prophecy, to another discerning of spirits, to another different kinds of tongues, to another the interpretation of tongues.
1 Corinthians 12:8-10 NKJV

1) "The word of wisdom." Wisdom is available to everyone who asks for it or seeks it.[4] The whole of Proverbs, for instance, is devoted to helping us gain practical wisdom and understanding for daily living. This accumulation of good sense and insight is akin to, but not exactly, what is meant by "the word of wisdom."

Solomon's most famous judgment gives us an example of this gift in operation. Having previously prayed for wisdom, God gave Solomon the perfect solution to a troubling dilemma: Which prostitute was the true mother of the child who died and which was lying. Solomon's decision in the case revealed to all Israel that that God was with him, giving wisdom.

Then the king answered and said, "Give the living child to the first woman, and by no means put him to death; she is his mother." And all Israel heard of the judgment that the king had rendered, and they stood in awe of the king, because they perceived that the wisdom of God was in him to do justice.
1 Kings 3:27-28

2) "The word of knowledge." This gift has a very strong prophetic component, giving "knowledge" to both the one who receives it and the one being ministered to that God is at work in a given situation. This elevates the faith level of everyone present for whatever it is that the Lord desires to do. Often, however, it doesn't seem like a word at all. In the context of a healing service it may be a sense of pain felt by the prayer minister in a very specific part of their body.

When that "word" is spoken out ("Someone here has ringing in their left ear that God wants to heal"), a person in the congregation with that condition will usually experience increased faith, often receiving healing as a direct result. When the blind man was told Jesus wanted to see him, his faith level was certainly enhanced. Jesus saw his response, noted the faith, and the healing happened.

> **And Jesus stopped and said, "Call him." And they called the blind man, saying to him, "Take heart. Get up; he is calling you." And throwing off his cloak, he sprang up and came to Jesus. And Jesus said to him, "What do you want me to do for you?" And the blind man said to him, "Rabbi, let me recover my sight." And Jesus said to him, "Go your way; your faith has made you well." And immediately he recovered his sight and followed him on the way.** Mark 10:49-52

3) "Faith." All who believe in Jesus have already received the gift of faith, so saving faith or faith in Christ's death and resurrection is not what is meant by this gift.[5] This gift conveys a supernaturally sustained ability to trust God in a specific situation or to believe for a specific thing that the Lord wants to accomplish. Persons who receive it don't have to work at believing God against what may seem like impossible odds.[6] They only have to make sure they don't lose what they have received.

Often this ability to believe for a specific thing is activated by a specific word quickened (made alive to you) from scripture or received directly from the Spirit. David's confident faith for killing Goliath seems to have been sustained by this kind of gift.

> **And David said, "The Lord who delivered me from the paw of the lion and from the paw of the bear will deliver me from the hand of this Philistine." And Saul said to David, "Go, and the Lord be with you!"**
> 1 Samuel 17:37

4) "Gifts of healings." There are so many things about us that can go wrong: physical sickness, systemic disease, organ failure, accidental injury, mental disease, and emotional wounds. It's no wonder that many "gifts" for "healings" are needed.

Everyone should pray for healing, all of us can seek to receive a greater capacity for effective prayer, but certain individuals have already been unquestionably gifted by the Lord for healing. Many of them are consciously aware of an anointing from the Lord which "signals" His presence upon them to heal someone. Sometimes it is a sensation of physical warmth on their hands; at other times it may be an ability to "see" faith upon someone, as with Paul in Lystra.

And in Lystra a certain man without strength in his feet was sitting, a cripple from his mother's womb, who had never walked. This man heard Paul speaking. Paul, observing him intently and seeing that he had faith to be healed, said with a loud voice, "Stand up straight on your feet!" And he leaped and walked. Acts 14:8-11 NKJV

5) "The working of miracles." Of course, sudden healings are miracles in themselves, but what is (likely) intended here are those activities of God which affect the natural order, not the human body—what are usually termed "signs and wonders" in the Hebrew scriptures.[7] Nature, too, can go awry. Jesus rebuked the wind for His disciples' sake. God stopped the mouths of lions for Daniel's sake. He also brought forth water from a rock and provided *mana* in the wilderness for His chosen people.

We, too, need miracles of all kinds in our lives: miracles of escape from imminent danger or looming debt; miracles of provision; miracles of deadly forces in nature stopped or turned aside. We have an awesome God-given ability to "speak" even to mountains, commanding nature just as Jesus did.

And he said to it, "May no fruit ever come from you again!" And the fig tree withered at once. When the disciples saw it, they marveled, saying, "How did the fig tree wither at once?" And Jesus answered them, "Truly, I say to you, if you have faith and do not doubt, you will not only do what has been done to the fig tree, but even if you say to this mountain, 'Be

taken up and thrown into the sea,' it will happen."
Matthew 21:19-21

6) "Prophecy." There are many levels to the prophetic. At the entry level is the kind of seeking we all do in prayer to find a word of encouragement or just the right book from an inspired author to match a friend's need. Jesus says that all of His sheep hear His voice. Some do more than others.

Those with a prophetic gift hear more frequently and more specifically from the Lord by means of a language of prophetic communication that may include dreams, visions, symbols and pictures, even more than words. This does not mean they get it right all of the time, but that they develop a dependable track record for accuracy which makes it worthwhile for others to pay attention to, weigh, and sift their sayings. Agabus' prophetic gift helped the church prepare for a famine.

> **Now in these days prophets came down from Jerusalem to Antioch. And one of them named Agabus stood up and foretold by the Spirit that there would be a great famine over all the world (this took place in the days of Claudius). So the disciples determined, everyone according to his ability, to send relief to the brothers living in Judea.** Acts 11:27-29

7) "Discerning of spirits." Having been active in the field of demonic deliverance, I can testify that there are at least two levels to the operation of this gift. There are some people (myself at times) who can discern by inward sense which demon needs to be cast out of a person, which spirits are oppressing a church or other organization, and even where angels or demons may be positioned around a room. There are others who have been given sight to see into the invisible realm that surrounds us all.

I have worked with many people who evidently had this ability, whose credibility and Christian character gave support to what they reported seeing. In battlefield conditions having someone with this gift is like having a spy behind enemy lines. To Balaam's chagrin, however, his donkey saw the angel blocking their path before he did. Nevertheless, it was a good thing he listened to what the donkey discerned.

> **And the donkey said to Balaam, "Am I not your donkey, on which you have ridden all your life long to this day? Is it my habit to treat you this way?" And he said, "No." Then the Lord opened the eyes of Balaam, and he saw the angel of the Lord standing in the way, with his drawn sword in his hand. And he bowed down and fell on his face.** Numbers 22:30-31

8) "Different kinds of tongues." In addition to "tongues" or languages that can be learned by the usual human means, there are tongues "of men and of angels" which are given by God for His own specific purposes.[8] On the day of Pentecost everyone in the Upper Room was baptized in the Holy Spirit and given an ability to speak human languages that they could not have previously known. This was a sign to the multitudes who heard them "speaking in their own tongue"—a convincing display of God's power which led to Peter's sermon and the conversion of 3000.[9]

There are also "tongues of angels" by which the Lord may be worshiped or entreated. These tongues have no human counterpart. The tongues spoken of here may be of either variety, but the setting is public worship, which is why it is stipulated that an interpretation should be given, something that is completely unnecessary if they are simply a part of the person's private prayer language. Such a setting requires interpretation for the sake of proclaiming the prophecy it contains.

> **Now I want you all to speak in tongues, but even more to prophesy. The one who prophesies is greater than the one who speaks in tongues, unless someone interprets, so that the church may be built up... So with yourselves, since you are eager for manifestations of the Spirit, strive to excel in building up the church.**
> 1 Corinthians 14:5, 12

9) "The interpretation of tongues." Interpreting tongues which are publicly uttered is necessary for the Lord to accomplish what the tongues describe. Without the interpretation coming forth, no one knows what was said. No one can even be confident that the tongues conveyed a message from the Lord or were initiated by Him, rather than from of the speaker's own soul.

This gets tricky really fast because the speaker has to have faith that someone is present who will be able to interpret what he/she believes God has prompted them to say (perhaps that will be themselves); likewise the interpreter has to have faith to believe that they are hearing from God at least enough of the message to launch out in faith to let it flow in fullness.[10]

Therefore, one who speaks in a tongue should pray for the power to interpret. 1 Corinthians 14:13

Learning about these gifts is not the same thing as doing them, but it is a necessary beginning. To go further you will need a fellowship of like-minded believers who are committed to discovering how to make themselves available to God, Jesus and the Holy Spirit at this level. You can be sure that there are others who are pursuing these things of God, as well as the Lord Himself. Passion for Jesus and compassion for others will carry anyone a long way towards the unfolding of every gift the Holy Spirit desires to release through us—if we don't set preconceived limits to what is possible. You can be sure that the Lord doesn't!

---

[1] Just as the Lord promised through Malachi, He opens windows in heaven and pours out a blessing. As great as the blessing on tithing is, the "outpouring" of the Spirit is even greater (see Chapter 7, "The Baptism of Power"): Malachi 3:10: *Bring the full tithes into the storehouse... I will... pour down for you a blessing until there is no more need.*

[2] The charismatic experience of the Corinthian church was by no means unusual. In the first two centuries of the church these nine operations of supernatural power flourished along with the baptism of the Spirit which enabled their widespread growth. The Early Church was fully charismatic across the whole Mediterranean basin! The rare exception would have been a church lacking in these two features as modern

---

scholarship has abundantly demonstrated. See Kilian McDonnel and George T. Montague, *Christian Initiation and Baptism in the Holy Spirit*, The Liturgical Press, Collegeville, Minnesota; 1990.

[3] Other gifts include the "ministerial" gifts or offices listed in Ephesians 4:11: apostles, prophets, evangelists, pastors, and teachers; the "motivational" gifts for service listed in Romans 12:6-8: prophesy, service, teaching, exhortation, giving, mercy, and administration; and gifts individually mentioned: hospitality, intercession, missionary, exorcism, music, craftsmanship, and celibacy. Even natural talents and abilities are gifts from God and can be placed under His leadership in service through Him to others. Ultimately, every good gift comes from the Father, so all genuine gifts have a spiritual Source and connection.

[4] James 1:5: *If any of you lacks wisdom, let him ask God… it will be given him.*

[5] Saving faith is described in Romans 10:13 and Ephesians 2:8-9: *By grace you have been saved through faith… not your own doing; it is the gift of God.*

[6] Jesus said that our primary "work" is to cultivate our faith—the gift of faith in Him that we have been given. It is understood by the Lord that most of our faith in Him (or for what He has promised to do) is something that we will have to work at maintaining: John 6:28-29: *This is the work of God, that you believe in him whom he has sent.*

[7] Two obvious exceptions to this sweeping general statement would be the raising of people out of death and the recreation of organs or other body parts, both of which have been occurring in our day in surprising numbers.

[8] 1 Corinthians 13:1: *If I speak in the tongues of men and of angels…*

[9] Acts 2:4-7: *They were bewildered, because each one was hearing them speak in his own language.*

[10] My friend, Eddy Browning, who brought me to the Lord had a dead-on prophetic gift as well as discerning of spirits (I had seven demons cast out of me the night of my conversion). It was his gift of tongues combined with the interpretation of tongues that came to my rescue many times in the early years of my growth in Christ. I would call Eddy on the phone and lay out my trouble; he would pray in tongues; then when the interpretation came, I was set free and fully satisfied I had heard from the Lord!

Doing Ministry

For it is God who works in you
both to will and to do of His good pleasure.
Philippians 2:13 MKJV

CHAPTER 9

DOING MINISTRY

There's nothing like doing the thing, especially when what we are doing is something we can be sure that Jesus is doing right along with us. The real Minister, the true Servant, is there on the inside wanting to get out into that hurting, lost world through us His chosen vessels. The secret to kingdom success is letting Him do ministry through you. It is also the secret to never becoming burned out.

For it is God who works in you, both to will and to work for his good pleasure. Philippians 2:13

Our Secret of Success

Success in ministry is learning to let Jesus work in you and through you. We need to let Him work in us so that He can work through us. On good days this can be as easy as child's play. When our trust, love and inward surrender are high, we hardly need any coaching from a book like this. We're good to go! At other times, however, it is as tough as nails. Why is that?

Because Jesus is in you, the Holy Spirit will lift and lead you into the many joys of working with Him, making you feel childlike and free.[1] Likewise, precisely because Jesus is in you, the enemy's camp will work steadily to oppose anything He might want to do through you. At those times you will feel hindered and besieged. Remember, too, that the Adversary doesn't just come at us from the outside; difficulties also arise from all that is still fallen within us. That's why we have to learn to let Jesus work *in* us, in order for Him to keep working through us.

There is no escaping this ongoing conflict. Just be ready for it. It is the inevitable cycle of our new life: struggle and victory, seed time and harvest, death to Self and resurrection with Christ.[2] Be encouraged: Opposition from the enemy is never wasted. God will always overturn it and use it to advance His work. In addition it often serves as the Lord's wash and wear cycle—something that He puts us through whenever we need to be cleansed of Self and liberated once again as glad-hearted, unencumbered children.[3]

We need this friendly work of the Lord in us because it is so easy to get caught up in trying to get results. Our desire to help people can easily be subverted by the enemy. We could focus on the problems and lose the peace of Christ, then press forward in our own strength until we've burned out the inner flame. Or, we might seize the reigns, trying to manage everything according to our own understanding and our own sense of timing. This always leads to frustration. Without even realizing it, by these and other ways we can take control of the work away from the Lord into our own hands. This never produces the desired results!

Success in ministry is letting Jesus have His way with us. His top priority is growing loving relationships—that's the key result He's looking for. Are we making the progress there that He desires? As for the work itself, it always goes better if Jesus is in the lead. He alone knows what He desires to accomplish and how to do it. The great thing about this is that He can be immensely pleased even with what may seem to us like miniscule gains, such as stopping what you're doing to give "a cup of water" to someone in need.[4]

Learning to follow Him is filled with unexpected moments of purpose and accomplishment when something vital (love, empathy, shared understanding) passes between us and the people we serve. Our service is also marked by times of quandary: Where did He go now? What was that about? What is He trying to teach me? Since so much depends upon Jesus doing His ministry through us, we need to understand and cooperate with this dynamic of the work.

The Source of Our Success

Jesus gathered the disciples on His last night with them for a final teaching on how to do ministry once He was gone. Just as they had always done ministry under His leadership while He was with them in the flesh, so now they were to make sure that He remained in charge once He was gone. But catch the wink: He wouldn't really be gone. He would remain with them as an abiding presence and He fully expected them (and us) to learn how to return the favor by learning to abide in Him. This teaching is so important that we need to study it in detail.

> **Abide in me, and I in you. As the branch cannot bear fruit by itself, unless it abides in the vine, neither can you, unless you abide in me. I am the vine; you are the branches. Whoever abides in me and I in him, he it is that bears much fruit, for apart from me you can do nothing. If anyone does not abide in me he is thrown**

away like a branch and withers; and the branches are gathered, thrown into the fire, and burned. If you abide in me, and my words abide in you, ask whatever you wish, and it will be done for you. <u>By this my Father is glorified, that you bear much fruit and so prove to be my disciples</u>. As the Father has loved me, so have I loved you. <u>Abide in my love</u>. If you keep my commandments, you will abide in my love, just as I have kept my Father's commandments and abide in his love. These things I have spoken to you, that my joy may be in you, and <u>that your joy may be full</u>... You did not choose me, but <u>I chose you and appointed you that you should go and bear fruit</u> and that your fruit should abide, so that <u>whatever you ask</u> the Father in my name, he may give it to you. John 15:4-11, 16

Our abiding is important to Jesus, as well as the fruit we are intended to bear. Unless we learn the way of abiding in Him we will be unable to bear *any* fruit. On the other hand, if we abide in Him, we will bear "much fruit." Bearing fruit glorifies the Father and proves that we are truly His disciples. The stakes are high! If we don't learn to abide in Him, we not only won't experience the overflow of His joy, we may actually risk being cast "into the fire." Indeed, we have been chosen that we "should go and bear fruit."

Fruit is what the branch (that's us) produces by abiding in the vine (that's Jesus). Fruit is not for the consumption of the branch, but for the nourishment of others. In the New Testament there are three basic kinds of fruit: the fruit of the Spirit,[5] the fruit of righteous living[6] and the fruit of advancing the kingdom.[7] We don't get to pick and choose among the fruit. Every one of us is called to cultivate all three kinds.

Notice the essential role of the fruit of the Spirit— peace, love, joy, patience, kindness, goodness, faithfulness, gentleness, and self-control. If we don't abide in Jesus, the fruit of the Spirit are the first to get spoiled! If we aren't bearing the fruit of the Spirit, whatever work we are doing will have a rotten smell to it. According to Paul, even if we have righteous deeds and kingdom advances to boast of, but have not love, then we "gain nothing."[8] Clearly, the fruit of the Spirit are essential to both life and ministry.

The Key to Our Success

Since abiding in Christ is the only way we can bear fruit, especially the fruit of the Spirit, then abiding is the key to doing ministry. In Jesus own words it is impossible to think of doing things for Jesus without also doing everything we can to abide in Him at the same time. It is not a question of one or the other. We do not get to choose between being active servants or being those who abide in Jesus. We must learn to do both! We have been chosen to "bear fruit" and it is only by abiding that we have any hope of accomplishing our assignment.

If this sounds impossibly hard, it is. We will never learn the way of abiding or of bearing true fruit unless Jesus helps us, but that is exactly what He wants to do. He says that whatever we ask for will be given us. Look what that promise means in this context. Anything we need in order to abide or bear fruit, God will gladly supply! Call on His Name—He will always come to your aid.[9] Return to Him as often as the peace of abiding departs—He will always welcome you back.[10] No one abides in Jesus all of the time. We all lose the peace He gives us, especially in the midst of trials. The great thing is recognizing that you have lost the peace of abiding (once again) and make a quick return!

Seen in this light, seeking to be of service to Jesus, presses us to learn how to abide in Him, and that in turn ushers in all of the inimitable joys of living in His presence.[11] Truly, His joy enters us as we learn to abide in Him. Once again Jesus demonstrates that His number one concern for us as servants is love: "abide in My love." From that place of strength, service becomes a joy and the fruit naturally follows.

Jesus overturns our natural bent. We may want success (results) at the work in order to feel confident we have pleased Him and don't mind striving and stressing to get those results. His approach is quite different. He is pleased if we take our confidence from trusting ourselves to His steadfast love. Then He gets to reap the results He wants through us *while we are trusting*.

Two Necessary Steps

How do we allow Jesus to do His ministry through us? Abiding is intimately connected with trusting Jesus for all He allows and obeying Him in what He asks. That is a subject all its own. Nevertheless, there are two steps we need to take at the beginning of any work of ministry. The first step is to consecrate the work to Him; the second step is to consecrate ourselves.

1) Consecrating the Work. We commit our field of service to Him in prayer. Christian work and prayer go hand in hand, because no amount of effort on our part can make up for any failure by us to bring the Lord in as the central player. Always keep in mind that it is His work in us and through us that will win the day. Naturally enough we pray for His blessing, but to ensure that, we commit the work to Him, asking Him to take charge over it and work with us to make sure that His will is done. The Holy Spirit will show what needs to be prayed for and help us with the prayers, but the central thing is truly committing or giving the work to God.[12]

2) Consecrating Ourselves. This needs doing up front in prayer, but it is necessary to keep watch over ourselves all along the way. The key to this is to intentionally place ourselves under His leadership through prayer and the yielding of our wills, just as He showed us was necessary for Him in the Garden: "Not my will, but Thine be done." Whenever we do this in life or in ministry, we have peace.[13] Any loss of peace is a clear call from the Holy Spirit to repent, return to the Lord, be refreshed in His presence and re-consecrate ourselves to operating under His leadership.[14]

---

[1] When faith in Christ is rising in us, all is glorious: Colossians 1:27: *The riches of the glory of this mystery, which is Christ in you, the hope of glory.*

[2] Paul describes this cycle in its extreme form: 2 Corinthians 4:11-12: *So death is at work in us, but life in you.*

[3] 1 Peter 5:6-7: *Casting all your anxieties on him, because he cares for you.*

[4] Notice how slight the action indicated by the Lord and how great His approval of it as a way of ministering of love: Mark 9:36-37: *Whoever receives one such child in my name receives me;* Mark 9:41: *Whoever gives you a cup of water to drink… will by no means lose his reward.*

[5] Galatians 5:22-23: *But the fruit of the Spirit is love, joy, peace, patience, kindness, goodness, faithfulness, gentleness, self-control…*

[6] Matthew 12:33-35: *The good person out of his good treasure brings forth good…*

[7] John 4:35-36: *Lift up your eyes, and see that the fields are white for harvest.*

[8] 1 Corinthians 13:1-3: *But have not love… I gain nothing.*

[9] Romans 10:13 *For "everyone who calls on the name of the Lord will be saved.*

[10] Hebrews 4:16: *Let us then with confidence draw near to the throne of grace…*

[11] Psalms 16:9: *In your presence there is fullness of joy…*

[12] In consecrating the work to the Lord, we should allow the Holy Spirit to examine our motives to ensure that our true desire is to serve the Lord, not any agenda of our own: Luke 16:13: *No servant can serve two masters…*

[13] Colossians 3:15: *And let the peace of Christ rule in your hearts…*

[14] Isaiah 30:15" *For thus said the Lord God, the Holy One of Israel, "In returning and rest you shall be saved; in quietness and in trust shall be your strength."*

CHAPTER 10

THE HEART OF A SERVANT

There are two sides to cultivating a servant's heart which we see fully revealed in Jesus. They also dove-tail beautifully into fulfilling the two commands He gave us. First, there is the passion to be about the Father's business which keeps us asking "What would You have me do?" This takes us upwards into God's heart and downwards into the humility that sets Self aside. Second, there is compassion which keeps us looking to the sea of humanity around us, listening for God's call that comes to us through their need.

"It shall not be so among you. But whoever would be great among you must be your servant, and whoever would be first among you must be your slave, even as the Son of Man came not to be served but to serve, and to give his life as a ransom for many." Matthew 20:26-28

The Lowest Place

Where would we be without those opportunistic sons of Zebedee, James and John? Their unabashed desire to one day sit enthroned beside Jesus, provoked the Lord to give us the penetrating look into His kingdom and His calling quoted above.[1] It's not our way, is it? He didn't come to make a name for Himself, or to get anything for Himself, or to be served by us. He came simply and solely to serve us, even to the ultimate end of laying down His life for us. He says that's what He wants us to be like.

With these few words Jesus stands the world on its head. Headship among us is characterized by making sure that others look up to our elevated position, bowing before us in gratitude, respect and obedience. We didn't climb all this way up the mountain for nothing! There's got to be something in it for us. Tragically, the very desire to rise to the top which lies behind so much of our excellence and achieving, comes from the lowest thing about us—our pride.[2] We don't have to rise very high to fall into this snare: Even the slightest elevation can have us looking to see if anyone else noticed our advance or being miffed if they didn't.

Jesus says that in His kingdom the head takes the lowest place.[3] Those who would follow Him must become like Him in being a servant to everyone else. You don't have to be the Pope or the President for this to apply to you. Moral greatness rests upon anyone who learns to be a servant. Those who seek leadership positions—"being first"—must be willing to descend even lower, becoming "slaves." Naturally enough, our own heads aren't going to take this self-debasement lying down! Fortunately, Jesus has given us a new heart, one just like His—the heart of a servant. Look no further: It is already in you, waiting and desiring to emerge.

And I will give you a new heart, and a new spirit I will put within you. And I will remove the heart of stone from your flesh and give you a heart of flesh. Ezekiel 36:26

Growing Your Heart

Our new hearts don't grow all by themselves. Like any tender young plant they require careful cultivation. The basic strategy is to plant your new heart in some field of service, keep watering it with the Word and with worship, and stand ready to pull weeds coming from your fallen nature when they show up. That won't take long. Inevitably, you will discover that there is a battle enjoined between the old ways of our fallen nature which seem so natural to us and the new ways of grace which are sometimes difficult to receive. This has been beautifully captured in song.[4]

Nature and Grace

By John Michael Talbot

Deep within me there lies a true distinction,
Between the things I would and what I really do.
I cannot believe that I am so unusual,
Isn't this the common sorrow within me and you?

Nature will seek only its own advantage.
It considers only how another might be used.
Grace will bring a new humility,
To comfort those afflicted and to help those once abused.

Nature might seek its fair consolation,
But it never offers its help without its price, without reward.
Grace finds reward in another's consolation,

Learning in this paradox the power of our Lord.

Nature will seek to be exalted in authority,
To argue its opinion and to have all the world conform.
Grace humbly comes in a silent assuredness,
Speaking only to conform a man unto His Lord.

Nature might seek its fair consolation,
But it never offers its help without its price, without
reward.
Grace finds reward in another's consolation,
Learning in this paradox the power of our Lord.

This heart of a servant within us doesn't seek recognition or reward. Its reward is to be of service. For that it is ever listening for the call, willing to set the demands of life or the desires of Self aside in order to respond to the One who has our ear.[5] Our new hearts live by the law of sacrifice just as Jesus did. [6] By dying to Self we enter into the greater joy of living for God. This new heart works beautifully when everything is going well. Few things give us more pleasure than serving in Jesus' Name. However, it should be evident that this new heart will have a lot of battles to fight, if it is going to triumph over the self-centered ways of our old nature.

If there was a short cut to eliminating Self, so that the new heart could truly flourish, Jesus would have told us. Instead, He warned us that we should be prepared to battle our selfish, self-centered side *daily*.[7] How can we go the distance with so demanding a task?

Going the Distance

The Old Testament gives us a vivid picture of a devoted servant whose love for his master inspired him to go the extra mile. Rather than take his leave when his indentured time was fulfilled, he chose to stay on as a permanent slave. Foreseeing that such a possibility could happen, the Lord made provision for it in His Word.

> **"Now these are the rules that you shall set before them. When you buy a Hebrew slave, he shall serve six years, and in the seventh he shall go out free, for nothing... But if the slave plainly says, 'I love my master, my wife, and my children; I will not go out free,' then his master shall bring him to God, and he shall bring him to the door or the doorpost. And his master shall bore his ear through with an awl, and he shall be his slave forever."**
> Exodus 21:1-2, 5-6

This may seem incredible to us, even unthinkable. That servant could have walked out a free man, owing nothing. Instead, He freely chose to become a "slave forever." Why? Masters in the ancient world provided food, clothing, bedding and personal security for their servants—the necessities of life. That could have been part of it, but we are simply told that he stayed for love. In a dramatic ceremony the "bond servant" was marked permanently as one whose ear would be forever attuned to his master's voice. He would be listening "at the door," whether he was to go outside on his master's business, or inside to attend to his master's personal requirements. His willingness to suffer and bleed sealed the covenant.

Amazingly, the first apostles referred to themselves in their letters as just such a bond servant. They even introduced themselves as "a bond servant of the Lord Jesus" before they mentioned (oh by the way) that they were also apostles chosen by God.[8] They evidently wanted the world to know that they were sold out to the One who had bought them at the price of His own Blood. Once saved, they could have chosen to live within the wide boundaries of the moral law, but they chose instead to enslave themselves to His will. They only wanted to come and go at His beck and call.

There is a significant difference between mere servants and bond servants. Good servants may still cherish and prefer their free time apart from doing their master's bidding. Bond servants seek only time at their master's side. Since our Master lives inside of us, this is surely the most searching form of slavery imaginable, with every thought, word and action coming under the scrutiny of our Lord's all pervasive presence. And yet, wonder of wonder, in His service we find our perfect freedom! God and Jesus only desire for us that which we ourselves would gladly choose if we had Their wisdom and foresight. Those who go deepest into loving service He raises highest into spiritual friendship.[9] The devoted servant and the kind-hearted Master are intimately intertwined—serving one another in love.

Two Motivations

We have not one, but two vast reservoirs of motivation for active service, whose ultimate source is in the heart of our God. It is, therefore, technically impossible to burn out or dry up if—and that is a really big *if*—you learn how to stay well-connected to Jesus. Seen in the right light, this provides extra incentive for staying active in ministry because serving others is one of those things that press us deeper into Christ, if we let it.[10]

1) Passion. Our first and most powerful source of motivation grows out of God's love for us and ours for Him.[11] This can be easily renewed whenever we return and rest our hearts in Him.[12] This is the secret of the bond servant. By always seeking to be at His side listening for our next assignment, there is a built-in reminder for staying refreshed by His presence.[13] Learning to walk step-by-step under the Lord's leadership ensures that we will spend our days seeking Him, because like Moses, we won't desire to go anywhere without His presence leading us.[14] You don't have to be especially good at this, just doggedly determined.[15]

2) Compassion. Our second source of motivation mirrors the Second Commandment that the Lord gave us: to love one another as we love ourselves. Provided that we have learned to accept and love ourselves, our hearts will naturally want to share with others the peace, joy and freedom that keep flooding into us. Because our passion for Jesus is filling our cup, we don't need to use people or get anything from them. We are free to serve them under His leadership, expecting nothing in return. It is enough to know that He knows. This is our baseline, but we can go deeper. We can want to see what He sees and feel what He feels when He looks into the lives around us. In this way our passion for Him, leads us into greater compassion for others.

Not only do we have these two passionate purposes to keep ourselves fired up for active service, we also have two monumental tasks: to take the liberating gospel out to the lost world and to carry loving compassion into the hurting world. That should keep us busy! But don't let busyness keep you from the most important part of it all: loving Jesus and loving the ones He loves. Growing a heart of love is our underlying purpose in ministry and our source of lasting joy. Gaining the heart of a servant will carry us a long way towards home.

---

[1] See Matthew 20:20-28 for the full passage.

[2] Lowest because most fallen. In rising upwards into unbridled pride, the Lucifer fell into the depths of depravity, becoming Satan, the one who opposes God.

[3] This is the paradox: He is our Head, but He also takes the lowest place of serving us, His Body: Colossians 1:17-18: *And he is the head of the body, the church…*

[4] John Michael Talbot has many CD's. The lyrics are powerful; the music is beautiful. "Nature and Grace" is on an album from his early period, *No Longer Strangers.*

---

[5] This is written about Jesus who now lives with this same desire on the inside of us: Hebrews 10:7: *Then I said, 'Behold, I have come to do your will, O God, as it is written.'*

[6] Hebrews 12:1-2: *Who for the joy that was set before him endured the cross…*

[7] Luke 9:23: *Let him deny himself and take up his cross daily and follow me.*

[8] See the letters of Paul (Romans, Galatians, Philippians, Colossians, and Titus), James, 2 Peter, and Jude. NKJV renders the title "bondservants."

[9] John 15:13-15: *No longer do I call you servants… but I have called you friends.*

[10] The "Big Five" connectors to Jesus are Bible, prayer, worship, fellowship and service. Do these regularly and the Lord will use them as "safety nets" to keep drawing you back to Himself whenever you stray, or to help hold you fast in case of an attack.

[11] If you feel your love for Him waning, go to Him to get it back. Our love for God is not a feeling that comes from us. It is what happens in us when we see His love: 1 John 4:19 AMP: *We love Him, because He first loved us.*

[12] Isaiah 30:15: *In returning and rest you shall be saved…*

[13] Acts 3:19: *Repent… that times of refreshing may come from the presence of the Lord.*

[14] Exodus 33:13-15: *If your presence will not go with me, do not bring us up from here.*

[15] I put that there for myself: I don't feel that I am especially good at anything I am pursuing, but I am doggedly determined to keep seeking Him for guidance and direction in all my ways. He blesses that right intention and seems to make up the difference. He will do the same for you!

CHAPTER 11

THE CARE OF SOULS

The people we pass every day on the streets will outlast the Grand Canyon and are of infinitely more worth than any governmental structure. How are we to handle them, especially when they come to us for ministry? Some are obviously stamped "Fragile, Handle with Care." Others have their secret life hidden further from sight. We can easily be like bulls in a china shop, if we don't take care with souls.

"So whatever you wish that others would do to you, do also to them, for this is the Law and the Prophets."
Matthew 7:12

Let "the Rule" Rule

Try as we might we will never be able to improve on this saying of the Lord. His Golden Rule could easily guide all of our efforts to minister to others. Just put yourself in their place and imagine how you would like to be treated. Imagine what you would be feeling; how you might be acting out; how you would be hoping that someone out there could sympathize and understand. Imagine how much an undeserved gesture of kindness or gentleness would mean to you. Would you want tender comfort? Or the truth kindly, but honestly spoken? Would you be grateful for anyone who could sense your pain? Or lift your spirits?

109

Without a doubt the Golden Rule should rule! But being the kind of folks that we are, we need clarification points to pin to our conscience so that we will recognize the moment when it is upon us. We are so secretly good at flipping the rule: expecting others to treat us as we want them to! Jesus never gave us permission to go at life that way. I have to treat them as I would want to be treated, but they are free to treat me however they like—I still have to treat them by the Rule.[1] So, let's resolve right at the beginning that we are going to live by the Lord's Rule even if others don't! Now for some points of further clarification.

Caring for Souls

Caring for souls primarily means taking care of their hearts.[2] You can feed a hungry homeless person a great meal, but if you treat them with disrespect, they will walk out emptier than when they came in. Similarly, you can minister to a hurting believer through prayers that have you both in tears, but if you tell others their secret, they will wish they never knew you. Here's a truth you can take to the bank: If the person needing ministry knew how to take care of their own heart, they wouldn't need you to minister to them. That's why we have to take such care with them. Their heart is what the Lord is after. Their heart is where He wants to dwell. Their heart is the key to all the other issues in their life.

Keep your heart with all diligence, for out of it spring the issues of life. Proverbs 4:23 NKJV

To care for others at the level of taking care of their hearts, means that we will have to attend to the needs of our own heart in the process. Jesus said that we should love others as we love ourselves.[3] This carries a subtle inference that the proper love of self is necessary for the proper love of others: We will love them as (to the extent that) we love ourselves. If accepting, forgiving and loving yourself as God loves you is hard for you, don't you imagine that hardness against yourself will get in the way of accepting, forgiving and loving others? Indeed it does! There is real help for this: please see "Love Thyself!" at our website for healing, healingstreamsusa.org.

In the meantime focus on this: the way that Jesus loves us is what we want to pass on to others. His love is what it's all about. This means that we will have to get very good (as we go along) at receiving His mercy and love, so that we will keep having a good supply of it to share with others.

I. Giving Comfort

One of the easiest things to do for others and certainly one of the most meaningful is to give comfort. As long as you keep in mind that giving comfort is not fixing them or fixing their situation, you will do well and you will be able to do it without getting stressed up. The problem comes when we just can't bear to see them suffering either so much or for so long. That's when we may succumb to the temptation to rescue them, putting the too-heavy burden of their life on our frail shoulders. Always remember that there is only

One Person who is fully qualified to do that. Look to see the part you can do (with His grace helping you) and *leave the really heavy lifting to Jesus.*

Job's friends are a classic example of people who started out giving comfort, but later gave in to the temptation to fix the problem which they mistakenly took to be Job himself. As long as they sat with him in silence sharing his pain, they did well. Moreover, there was nothing back-breaking about the assignment. It comes naturally to us to "weep with those who weep."[4] They blew it, however, when they lost patience both with Job (who was becoming a pill) and with the Lord (who wasn't acting fast enough to resolve things). If all you can think to do is commiserate with and befriend the hurting person that is all you need to do. Beyond this, it often helps to remember how the Lord brought genuine comfort to you in a similar situation and see if that shows you some further part you can play.

> **Blessed be the God and Father of our Lord Jesus Christ, the Father of mercies and God of all comfort, who comforts us in all our affliction, so that we may be able to comfort those who are in any affliction, with the comfort with which we ourselves are comforted by God.**
> 2 Corinthians 1:3-4

II. Guarding Confidence

It is safe to say that no one will have any confidence in us if we cannot keep a confidence that they share with us. Don't think just in terms of secrets that may be shared in confessional moments. These certainly must be guarded with the utmost concern for their privacy.

However, there are many things of an intimate nature that may come to our attention when ministering to others: the way they look or how they behave; the way their house looks; their family relationships or financial situation. Whatever comfort the Lord may give them through us will be stripped away if we don't guard these privileged glimpses into their lives.

People who are suffering pain or lack are already humbled and vulnerable if they have sought others out for help. In a very real sense they are standing before us with their naked need exposed. Nakedness in scripture represents that which would give us shame if openly displayed. Think of Adam and Eve instinctively reaching for those fig leaves. Paul wrote that just as we treat our "unpresentable parts" with greater modesty, so in the Body of Christ we are meant to clothe the weaker members with greater honor, taking care to guard their dignity.[5] Furthermore, it seems that the Lord took a dim view of Noah's son who exposed his father's "nakedness"—even though Noah had behaved in a disreputable way.[6] When in doubt, keep quiet about it.

> **Never repeat what you are told and you will come to no harm; whether to friend or foe, do not talk about it, unless it would be sinful not to, do not reveal it; you would be heard out, then mistrusted, and in due course you would be hated. Have you heard something? Let it die with you. Courage! It will not burst you!**
> Ecclesiasticus 19:7-10 TJB (the Apocrypha)

III. Genuine Courtesy

The rules of etiquette and the traditional courtesies originated as ways for showing respect to others.[7] They still work. Key among these is the willingness to take the time to look people in the eyes, to listen carefully to what they are saying and to share empathetically with their plight. This goes a long ways towards helping them. Not only does it enable you to access their situation more accurately (so that you can give better care), but it immediately gives them the comfort of being treated with dignity, as someone who is worth your time. The care of souls and an assembly line approach to solving human problems are completely incompatible! If you put people on the clock they always know it, and feel diminished. It is a breach of common courtesy.

No one exhibited the divine grace that lies within genuine courtesy better than St. Francis of Assisi. Be sure to read about him when you have time and if you don't have time, make time.[8] He was called "the mirror of perfection" in his day—the medieval world marveled at the ways Jesus shined out through his every word or deed. He made it a point of personal honor never to meet anyone who was poorer than himself. This kept his brother monks busy finding better things for him to wear because he was forever exchanging his garments with every beggar he met. Let that image penetrate you: The heart of courtesy is to treat other souls as if they matter more to you than your own immediate comfort.

So if there is any encouragement in Christ, any comfort from love, any participation in the Spirit, any affection

and sympathy, complete my joy by being of the same mind, having the same love, being in full accord and of one mind. Do nothing from rivalry or conceit, but in humility count others more significant than yourselves. Let each of you look not only to his own interests, but also to the interests of others. Philippians 2:1-4

---

[1] Obviously, I'm not suggesting that they should be allowed to do illegal things to us, like assault us, or steal from us. But verbal abuse? At our mission (the Old Savannah City Mission in Savannah, GA) we reign in abusive and offensive language, but we work at not letting it get to us; otherwise, we would be going off on them! Jesus said that there is a blessing to reap when we are verbally abused. It is well worth learning how to reap: Matthew 5:11-12: *Blessed are you when others revile you and persecute you and utter all kinds of evil against you falsely on my account.*

[2] "Soul" is a term that has wide and rich usage in the Bible, but no clearly established definition. General agreement has it that we are spirit, soul and body and that the soul is composed of intellect, emotion and will. The heart is the deepest part of the soul.

[3] Mark 12:31: *The second is this: 'You shall love your neighbor as yourself.'*

[4] Scripture is clear that this is what we are meant to do by way of comforting others: Romans 12:15-16: *Rejoice with those who rejoice, weep with those who weep...*

[5] 1 Corinthians 12:22-26: *But God has so composed the body, giving greater honor to the part that lacked it... but that the members may have the same care for one another.*

[6] Two brothers were praised for covering their father's nakedness: Genesis 9:20-23: *Shem and Japheth... Their faces were turned backward, and they did not see their father's nakedness.*

[7] Showing respect is very Biblical: Romans 13:7: *Pay to all what is owed to them... respect to whom respect is owed, honor to whom honor is owed.*

[8] Many books have been written about St. Francis, but the best is a collection made shortly after he died. Part history, part fable, you have to do a bit of sorting it out, but the images it gives us of this remarkable man are indelible: *The Little Flowers of St. Francis.*

CHAPTER 12

THE ART OF LISTENING

Hearing what people say is one thing. Really listening is something else entirely. What turns listening into an art form is learning how to juggle listening to others and listening for the Lord at the same time. Listen well enough to others and you will more easily hear from the Lord. These simple rules and visual images will help put you on track, but only practice makes perfect.

And he said, "He who has ears to hear, let him hear."
Mark 4:9

A Lost Art

Sometime in the last century we lost the art of letter writing. Once widespread and flourishing, writing long, thoughtful letters by hand kept people intimately in touch over great distances, but the telephone and air travel supplanted it. Something similar seems to be happening to story tellers and good listeners. Where are the raconteurs who could hold you spell bound with a simple tale lovingly told? Where are the caring souls who set their lives aside to really give a good listen to yours? It seems as if both are being crowded out by the pressured pace of modern life, for both of these art forms require a gracious supply of time in which to thrive.

This cultural deficit actually makes our task as Christian ministers much easier. So many people are weighted down or stressed up with the burdens they are carrying. Often their attempts to find a caring soul have been brushed off by people too busy to give them the time of day. Others they encountered were so filled with their own cares they didn't dare open themselves to feeling the weight of another's concern. And then there were false friends who heard them out, but failed to keep the confidence. In such a cultural climate finding a good listener is a rare treasure indeed! Yet, listening is the easiest point of access for those who desire to enter into the care of souls which is the essence of Christian ministry.

The beautiful thing about becoming a good listener is a) that you can start right away and b) you can easily do a lot of good and very little harm.[1] The deeper you go into Christian ministry the more training you will need and the more danger there will be of inadvertently causing damage. If you want to counsel people, or exercise a gift of prophecy, or minister inner healing and deliverance, you'll have to strap yourself in for the long haul. Seeking to help people at the level of their deepest need requires training and teamwork.[2] But if you want to relieve people by listening well, all you need is one good ear. If you have two, so much the better!

Ears to Hear Him

Listening is also important because our life with God is predicated upon listening carefully. In fact our ability to listen to others will increase dramatically as we learn how to give ear to the Lord. He speaks His word to us in a variety of ways. We listen for what He may be saying to us through scripture, through the words of others, through books, through conscience and through the way the Spirit guides our circumstances. That's a lot of listening! But that is not all.

There is an art to listening to the Lord. If you stay busy, you hear very little. The more you slow down, the more you notice that He just might be trying to get your attention about something. Then, if you really settle down and get quiet, you just might (finally) be in the right position to hear what He is saying. Imagine a darkened, windswept, rain-splattered pond. If an acorn were to drop on the surface you'd hardly notice. However, let that same pond be utterly still on a sunny day and anything dropped on the surface will be immediately heard and its effects seen across the whole expanse of quiet water. Learn to be that quiet pond on the inside and you will hear so much better from the Lord. How will we ever understand our lives or our world, if we don't pause to really hear Him when He speaks?

And he called the people to him and said to them, "Hear and understand." Matthew 15:10

All of this training at listening to the Lord comes in handy when listening to people. With them also it is not just a simple matter of recognizing and understanding words. The way they speak, their choice of words, their inflections, pauses and points of emphasis all give insight into their inner conversation—the thoughts of their heart. Body language and facial expressions also send a message, sometimes more loudly than anything they may actually be saying. If a person looks really down and discouraged and you hear it in their voice, but they tell you "all's well," what are you going to listen to as truth?

Just as we need to be quiet to hear from the Lord, so too we need to be quiet to listen well to others. Being unquiet on the inside always gets in the way of good listening. Haven't we all seen people at parties who can't wait for the other person to finish speaking, so they can jump in? Many people, when introduced to someone new, are so anxious what to say that they don't hear and remember the person's name. Or, perhaps something you heard triggered a very distracting thought. By the time you came to the end of it, you looked up and realized the other person was still speaking to you! These are just a few examples to show the need for emptying out as soon as you turn your attention to someone who wants to open up to you.

Stop, Look and Listen

We have to be ready to give our complete attention at a moment's notice. Years ago we had railroad signs in this country which said, "Railroad Crossing: Stop, Look and Listen." If you don't want to wreck the other person's train of thought, let this bygone phrase remind you of the danger of not coming to a full stop! Then, let the whole phrase provide a framework for excellent listening.

I. Stop!

As soon as you see that someone wants to open up to you, or has a legitimate need to talk, stop what you're doing. This should be obvious, but the devil is in the details. If you look at your watch, or fidget, or show the slightest sign of irritation or impatience, you may lose your moment with them. Come to a full stop and *stay* stopped. Set the stuff in you aside. Don't start thinking of other things you could be doing, unless of course, you should be doing them. In that case it is better to listen well to the first few sentences, explain that you have to go, but would really like to hear more later. Honesty like this will save you from resentment and them from embarrassment.

Inconvenience, on the other hand, can conceal the call of the Lord. Moses famously turned aside upon seeing the burning bush—it wasn't his plan.[3] Had he not noticed and stopped, he could easily have missed out on joining the Lord in a very heroic part of the Rescue. If you don't know it yet, you may as well brace yourself for finding it out soon: The Lord takes a rather cavalier attitude towards our agendas.[4] He prefers His plans to ours! Imagine. This means that your burning bush moments with others may come at seemingly inopportune times. Take time to tune in to the Lord. Lift the interruption immediately up to Him. If you can't honorably set it aside, set your agenda aside instead. He'll help you with that later.

II. Look!

Above all, look them in the eyes. Look with your heart of love and acceptance that Jesus gives you.[5] Look to see how important this moment is to them. Just don't overwhelm them by too intense a gaze—people in need often feel insecure and wilt if you look into them too deeply or too long. Then, as you have opportunity, take in the whole aspect of the person to see what that might tell you as you begin listening to them. Are they in a pain or a panic? Do they seem distressed and disheveled? Do they look like they need an immediate response from you to calm them down? How badly do they seem to be in need? Will someone else have to be called in, or does this seem like something you (with the Lord's help) can handle?

While you're looking, look around. Is this a good place for the person to open up? Will it afford them enough privacy? Do they seem on the brink of tears? In that case is there a quieter corner or more convenient place for the conversation? If you are feeling self-conscious or awkward about being approached, try not to let it show. Above all, never worry how the situation will look to others. Deal with those feelings immediately by looking up to the Lord and seeing or sensing if you have a green light from Him to go forward in this location. That's all that matters. Very likely you will get the go ahead, since the burning bush moment is already a sign of His Providence in choosing the time and place. If not, suggest a better location and move there.

III. Listen!

James tells us to be quick to listen, slow to speak.[6] That's our guide. Affirm their feelings, not necessarily their opinions. Wait patiently for your time to speak— don't interrupt. Be willing to count your own words as small things compared to what the Lord will be speaking to them, simply by you listening well. The image here is of a full pitcher of water. They are filled to the brim with all kinds of thoughts and feelings. If they don't tell someone they will overflow!

Your job is to let them pour what's inside them out upon your listening ears. It hardly matters where they begin. Their heart will secretly direct their conversation to the points that really matter. That's where you want to focus your innermost attention: on whatever it is that their heart is seeking to express. Don't strain. Just listen to them and to the Lord. If some insight needs to come to you, it will. Once that comes out into the open, your own heart will help you give the right response when it's your turn to speak. If you can find nothing significant to share, don't reproach yourself. Keep listening! Turning on the lights for you and your friend is the Lord's job. We are wisest when we wait on Him to do just that.

In the meantime, remember that we weep with those who weep and laugh with those who laugh. Both are healing.[7] Just go with the flow at first, responding to them as Jesus does with you. Set aside any judgments that may arise against their situation or their behavior. Ask questions if need be to keep the flow going: "What hurts? How did that make you feel?" Be a spiritual sponge! Absorb what they are sharing, taking it to your own heart and holding it up to the Lord in prayer. Be directive or assertive only if they seem to be straying off focus or dodging something. Good listening creates a bond of trust. You have to earn the right to speak.

As they empty out, this give you the opportunity to pour in some encouragement or the wisdom gained from a similar experience.[8] Just don't be in a hurry to do that. The quarry is dove like. If you don't quietly wait for your moment, you may startle them into taking flight. The primary comfort is not your words, but your love. That is shown incredibly well by listening well. It is rightly said that a burden shared is half lifted—and you don't even have to do any of the lifting. The Lord will lift their spirit through the principle of fellowship.

Hospitality to Strangers

Good listening is a way of showing "hospitality to strangers."[9] Perhaps you already know them to some degree. Nevertheless, their problems reveal an inner depth and strangeness—the fundamental *estrangement* from God and others that all of us suffer from in one way or another. By listening well you are welcoming them into your presence and treating their conversation with the respect a guest of your house deserves. God will use your caring and listening heart to bring much comfort and restoration, even if you have no inspired insight to give. Just by talking out loud people are helped, even to the point of discovering the answer for themselves. Just know your limits. Avoid sharing about unhealed, wounded areas in your life and getting in too deep into theirs. Follow these simple guidelines and you will not only do others a great deal of good, you will be making friends for eternity as you go along.

---

[1] Hippocrates, the father of Western medicine, included in the famous "Hippocratic Oath" that all doctors take a promise to do no harm: "With regard to healing the sick, I will devise and order for them the best diet, according to my judgment and means; and I will take care that they suffer no hurt or damage."

[2] Even so, being a good listener is essential for becoming good in any other area of ministry.

[3] See Exodus 3:1-4:17 for the complete story.

[4] James 4:13-15: *Say, "If the Lord wills, we will live and do this or that."*

[5] Romans 5:4-5: *God's love has been poured into our hearts through the Holy Spirit.*

[6] James 1:19-20: *Let every person be quick to hear, slow to speak, slow to anger...*

[7] Romans 12:15-16: *Rejoice with those who rejoice, weep with those who weep...*

[8] 2 Corinthians 1:3-5: *So that we may be able to comfort those who are in any affliction, with the comfort with which we ourselves are comforted by God.*

[9] Hebrews 13:1-2: *Do not neglect to show hospitality to strangers...*

CHAPTER 13

INNER HEALING AND DELIVERANCE

Basic discipleship enables us to prune the bad fruit off of our spiritual tree by calling on Jesus in any moment of need. Inner healing and deliverance are needed to pull out our deeply buried root issues. We all have them. They are unresolved stuff still stuck in us that produce bumper crops of bad attitudes and actions. As the saying goes, "Where's there's fruit, there's a root." The great thing is that once you deal with the root, a lot a bad fruit goes away.

> "I am the true vine, and my Father is the vinedresser. Every branch of mine that does not bear fruit he takes away, and every branch that does bear fruit he prunes, that it may bear more fruit." John 15:1-2

Issues Rooted in the Past

Inner healing and deliverance pick up where basic discipleship leaves off. In a sense we go below ground to get at the root issues causing spiritual problems (sins) or emotional pain (wounds). Where basic discipleship is about pruning away the bad fruit that shows up on your spiritual tree in present moments, inner healing goes after the past issues where deeply buried roots feed the rotten fruit on the surface.

See to it that no one fails to obtain the grace of God; that no "root of bitterness" springs up and causes trouble, and by it many become defiled. Hebrews 12:15

Before we start it needs to be said that this chapter is in no way intended to be a training manual for doing deep works of inner healing or deliverance as a lone wolf. It takes being a part of a team. It takes being mentored by others. It takes a good deal of time invested in training. The disciples spent three years with Jesus, watching how He did what He did, listening to all His messages and getting their questions answered by the Master. Then He left them to it as a Body of believers. *Don't try this on your own!* Remember the sad case of the seven sons of Sceva who fled "naked and bruised" when a deliverance session went south.[1.]

That being said there are entry levels to inner healing that any Christian can do which will help others find healing for some (not all) of the issues that trouble them. That's the work of The Keys (see the Glossary below and Chapter 15). For now, however, let's content ourselves with understanding the basics. Jesus said that if we would continue in His Word, we would know the truth and the truth would make us free. Being "made free" by learning the truth is a process, but it is also a battle.

So Jesus said to the Jews who had believed in him, "If you abide in my word, you are truly my disciples, and you will know the truth, and the truth will set you free." John 8:31-32

As we fight the good fight of faith to believe that God's truth really is the truth, then healing goes forward. Emotional and spiritual healing is a truth encounter far more than it is a power encounter. Although demons can and must be driven out by the power of Jesus' Name,[2] spiritual darkness is first and foremost a lie.[3] Believing lies gives darkness its power. As Rolland Baker says, "It was untruth that broke the world. God is using truth to mend it."[4]

Inner healing is essentially replacing the lies of the enemy with truths from Jesus. Whenever this is successfully accomplished, evil spirits lose their right to remain. Doing deliverance is almost always feather light whenever inner healing has gone before it. Sometimes, however, deliverance has to come first, because the person is so tormented that they cannot process truth sufficiently to work on their inner life. These can be knock-down, drag-out sessions and if you're not fully equipped and covered in prayer, you just might be the one knocked down! Know your limits. Once the spirits are cast out, inner healing should be ministered so that the person can be fully on board with whatever they will need to do to stay free in the future.

Glossary of Terms

1) Issues, Wounds and Scars. Issues are the bumps, bruises and scrapes of the emotional life which we shoved down and never really released at the time they happened. Everyone has them and most of the time they can be easily mended by The Keys. Issues are memories of people or events that come bobbing

129

up to the surface like tissues in a box. Like tissues they can be dealt with one at a time—pull it all the way up and out and give it to God. Just know that other issues are sure to appear!

Wounds, on the other hand, are issues that carried us deeper into emotional trauma at the time the event occurred. The pain is still intensely active. Wounds are usually infected with lies that the enemy sowed into them and were further complicated by our own ungodly reactions. Nevertheless, they can be completely healed. It just takes more time, attention and determination to fully cleanse the wound and see it healed.[5]

Scars are healed wounds. Simple issues don't leave scars, but wounds do. We can be so completely mended that there is no pain left in the memory, yet we have been marked by what we passed through. Wear your scars as a badge of honor. You not only survived an attack of the enemy, you have gained wisdom, an enlarged heart and a living testimony of the Lord's ability to heal deep wounds. That's a tremendous encouragement to others.

2) Strongholds. These are un-surrendered, un-healed or un-crucified areas of the old nature embedded in our flesh. Whenever we are touched by people or events in a certain way the stronghold springs to life. The negative emotion it represents gets a strong hold on us, making it extremely difficult to break free before our inward thoughts or feelings become words and actions we will regret later.

Strongholds are habit patterns of thought and belief that have become ingrained in us by past repetitions. We've always reacted that way! Now, that the Lord is calling for a different response, the stronghold tries to jump in first and block the way, often without any conscious decision on our part. Strong, but wrong, emotional reactions have to be carried as captives to Christ.[6] Then the inner lie that they are built upon can be held up to the light of His truth and renounced.

3) Ministering the Keys. Jesus promised that He would give us the "keys of the kingdom" to all who, like Peter, apprehend by faith who He really is.[7] There are many keys that Jesus gives us which work to unlock our destiny, release the supernatural workings of the Spirit, or lead to fruitfulness in service. These three keys unlock the heart.

The first key is getting really, really good at receiving His forgiveness, so good that there is no shame or blame, regret, guilt, or condemnation left in any of our memories of past sin and sinfulness. That's true freedom! The second key is turning right around and setting free everyone who has ever done anything against you or your loved ones by forgiving them fully from the heart. Once done, there is no pain left in the memory. What an incentive!

The third key is believing God's truth, especially the truth of His promises, so fully that there is no anxiety or despair left in you, only peace, freedom and joy. That really frees your heart to soar like an eagle. These keys are a vital part of basic discipleship. We need to use them on every present moment that triggers any negative emotional response in us. But they also work splendidly on issues rooted in the past. You can't do inner healing without them. They are at the core of what is needed to free us from pain and bondage coming from either the present or the past.

4) Inner Vows. These are the misguided attempts people make to deal with the pain or injustice they experienced, usually in childhood. The son of an alcoholic father may vow, "I will never be like my dad!" only to discover later on that the pattern is thoroughly entrenched. In trying to break generational sin patterns or correct our own behavior, we inadvertently put the weight of transformation on our own shoulders. Here, the problem is not so much getting free of inner vows and the bitter judgments that go with them, as in remembering them or recognizing them for what they are. Once identified, they can be fairly easily renounced and broken. Until then, they are a secret source of stronghold power working against true liberty of spirit.

5) Ungodly Beliefs. At the heart of our negative emotions are ungodly beliefs engendering them. Why does anyone want to curse out someone who hurt their feelings? Because sometime in the past they began deeply believing that it is the right way to handle that kind of situation. Why does anyone crave a substance? Because there is a tenaciously held belief that that the fix is going to do them some good. It may be that an evil spirit is pressing its own twisted emotions on us at times, forcing us feel what it feels, but if we cling to a right belief we can resist any wrong feeling until it leaves.

Ungodly beliefs compromise our ability to discern right from wrong. They feed negative emotions and weaken our ability to resist temptations from the enemy. Ungodly beliefs form the core of any stronghold. These must be carried as captives to Christ, repented of and renounced, breaking all agreements with the enemy. Then the truth can be confessed and believed to the liberation of the new emotional responses the Holy Spirit brings.

6) Healing of Memories. Nothing can change the past. Nothing needs to change our memories of it, if what we are remembering actually happened. What brings healing is to let our memories become infused with heaven's perspective, so that the painful way we had been remembering something is expanded by greater truths we were unaware of at the time. In this way "death is swallowed up in victory."[8] For instance, a person may have been traumatized thinking that they were abandoned by their family or friends at a time when the enemy did his best to destroy them. Let the perspective radically shift. See by faith that the invisible God was doing His best to protect life, even when the enemy was doing his worst. They were never abandoned; otherwise they would be dead! This shift is by no means easy to accomplish, but when it happens the memory tells an entirely different story: We are survivors; we are loved; we are saved—even when we were most vulnerable—because our loving Father chose to rescue us.

Memories can be healed just as ungodly beliefs are healed by renouncing the lying message ("No one cared!") and choosing to believe the truth ("God was with me!"). This way of healing memories works like a champ, but only if the person has a muscular faith and well-exercised prayer life of their own. As a mercy to our weakness, the Lord provides a second way of healing memories—by entering into them Himself and bringing a perspective that shifts both mind and heart. This is not guided imagery, nor should it ever be taken in that direction. We are not telling the Lord what to do or trying to make the individual see what we think they should see. The truth is that Jesus really was there *then* and He is here *now*. What would He have liked to show you or do for you, if you had eyes to see Him back then? There is no guarantee that Jesus will show up in the person's memory, but if He does, the painful event is always transformed by something He reveals.

7) Curses and Generational Sin. Generational sins[9] are the primary impact of the curse of the Law[10] upon the average person, until they reach an age where their own wrong choices and consequences catch up with them. Every family has its flaws: Certainly no one is perfect at not sinning, or even perfect at repenting. So, family systems pass on a pattern of sins from one generation to another, until someone rises up who says, "It ends here!" It is easy to see the flaw, especially if it has deeply wounded you, but what's needed is the compassion to plead mercy, grace and forgiveness over the ones who brought the curse into your life. Then repentance for the whole family line, pleading the Blood of Jesus and declaring the curse to be broken—nailed to the cross[11]—will bring deliverance, if they are combined with a steely determination to put that sin to death in your own life. Let us take our stand with mighty Joshua who declared, "As for me and my house, we will follow the Lord."[12]

Breaking curses off a person that have been placed on them by another, follows a similar pattern and is relatively simple. However, breaking the deep curse of occult involvement requires taking things to a greater level of intensity, especially if the bondage or emotional destruction was severe. In such cases every aspect of inner healing and deliverance will be required. As described in scripture the occult encompasses four main categories: the worship of false gods (idol worship; false religions), forbidden ways of seeking knowledge of the future (astrology, fortune telling), forbidden contact with the dead (séances, mediums), and forbidden ways of seeking to access spiritual power (witchcraft, sorcery). Freedom is real, but so are the powers of darkness. Never enter into this lightly!

8) Deliverance from Oppression. Evil spirits come in all shapes and sizes. They also have different assignments and personalities. Scripture speaks of spirits of fear, lying spirits, a spirit of jealousy, and a spirit of heaviness, among others.[13] It just may be that every sin mentioned in scripture has an evil spirit assigned to inflict that sin upon us. However, our negative emotions are not the same thing as evil spirits, any more than symptoms of physical sickness are. Nevertheless, the dark kingdom stands somehow behind the flare ups of disease in our bodies and the *dis*-ease in our souls.

Whenever we give ground to the enemy, emotional strongholds can be formed by our agreements with ungodly beliefs that match his own demented perspective. Let those strongholds grow unchecked and a tipping point may be reached where an evil spirit begins oppressing us. Whenever that happens, a spirit of fear (for instance) can throw us into a panic attack or hammer us with anxiety anytime it wants to—because we have lost the ability to discern the danger and resist its pressure. Inner healing can undercut the power of any evil spirit, leaving it no ground to stand upon, if the person is able to cooperate. If not deliverance can bring freedom, but inner healing will still be needed to maintain it.

9) Deliverance from Possession. You're not ready for this, so don't even think about it. Probably no one is. It is only by the grace of God that some can minister freedom to those who are this deeply bound to darkness. Fortunately, it is extremely rare, compared to all the other problems that people have. Possession simply means that an evil spirit is in such complete control ("possession") of the person that they vanish from sight—all you see and hear is coming directly from the enemy.

There is a debate going on about whether Christians can actually be possessed by the enemy, since we are the Lord's possession.[14] The truth is that Christians can be so oppressed that the enemy can manifest directly through them. They may not be fully possessed in the same way that an unbeliever might be, but when manifestations are going on there is virtually no visible difference.

Let the caution be repeated: Having head knowledge of these terms and a zeal to be about it, does not quality anyone for doing ministry at this level. You will certainly do more harm than good, if you do not submit to being trained by others who have gained practical experience and have the wisdom and patience to work with you. Pioneers are needed in every field to open up new territory when no one has gone before. Those pioneers have already come and opened this field in the preceding decades. The rest of us have been learning from them or from their books.[15] Once you get trained, let's hope that on-the-job training will take you further than the pioneers went, but don't presume you can outdistance them without studying them first. Take time to enjoy the adventure of learning!

---

[1] Acts 19:13-16: *And the man in whom was the evil spirit leaped on them, mastered all of them and overpowered them, so that they fled out of that house naked and wounded.*

[2] Mark 16:17: *In my name they will cast out demons.*

[3] John 8:44: *The devil… for he is a liar and the father of lies.*

[4] Visitation Conference message given in March 2006, Columbia, SC. by Rolland Baker, Mozambique missionary. Conference notes.

[5] The Lord doesn't want us to gloss over these wounds, healing them "lightly" with only an encouraging word: Jeremiah 8:10: *Saying, 'Peace, peace,' when there is no peace.*

[6] We are not "to blame" for any emotional reaction we may have, but we are responsible for what we choose to do with. The responsible thing is to carry it to Christ and deal with it His way: 2 Corinthians 10:4-6: *And take every thought captive to obey Christ.*

[7] Non-Catholics generally believe that the keys were not given exclusively to Peter, but to all who receive the same revelation he did: Matthew 16:16-19: *Peter replied, "You are the Christ, the Son of the living God." And Jesus answered... I will give you the keys...*

[8] This passage is about eternal life, but it gives expression to the way that heaven triumphs over the earthly by overwhelming it: 1 Corinthians 15:54-55: *When the perishable puts on the imperishable, and the mortal puts on immortality, then shall come to pass the saying...*

[9] Exodus 34:6-7: *Visiting the iniquity of the fathers...to the third and the fourth generation.*

[10] Deuteronomy 27:26: *Cursed be anyone who does not confirm the words of this law...*

[11] Galatians 3:13-14: *Christ redeemed us from the curse of the law by becoming a curse for us.*

[12] Joshua 24:15: *But as for me and my house, we will serve the Lord.*

[13] See 2 Timothy 1:7; 1 Kings 22:22; Numbers 5:30; Isaiah 61:3

[14] Exodus 19:5-6: *You shall be my treasured possession among all peoples*; 1 Corinthians 6:19-20: *You are not your own, for you were bought with a price.*

[15] Pioneers in inner healing include Agnes Sanford, John and Paula Sanford, Rita Bennett, Francis and Judith McNutt, and Leanne Payne. Pioneers in deliverance include Don Basham, Derek Prince, Neil Anderson, and Rebecca Brown

CHAPTER 14

GIVING TALKS

There is one rule that governs all talks: Make sure you have something to say. This book can't help you with that (unless you want to use these materials—please do!), but it can supply the coaching for how to know when you've got something to say and what to do with it when you do.

May my teaching drop as the rain, my speech distill as the dew, like gentle rain upon the tender grass, and like showers upon the herb. Deuteronomy 32:2

The Goal of a Good Talk

The goal is not primarily to give a good talk. Don't focus on that. The goal is to get some truth, some message that is really important to you across to them. Just make sure that you believe it with all of your heart and that you see why it liberates you to believe it.[1] Then you will want them to get it as much as you have. This actually frees you from being self focused and sets your heart on fire to share a truth that is burning inside you to be expressed. So get your passion and clarity up about what you want to share and let it become so important to you that it drowns out pestering concerns for how the message (and you) will be received.

Philips Brooks, a highly regarded preacher of the 19th century, wrote that we should teach truth, not just so people will know it, but so that they will be saved by believing it.[2] You will communicate effectively what you are passionate about them getting! Know and be convinced of what they need to get out of your teaching and they will naturally want to pay attention. Brooks also said that all good preaching or teaching is eternal truth brought through human personality. Never strain at this. The more natural, simple and genuine you are, the more you will truly be yourself as the Lord created you to be—and your teaching will be all the better for it. Don't compare yourself to others. Just fall in love with Jesus, then love the truth He has given you to share, then get yourself out of the way, and share it like there's no tomorrow.[3] The real you will come through along with the His truth. Both will be a blessing.

Elements of a Good Talk

I. The Core Message

The core message is like bones in our body. It gives strength and unity to the whole talk. Everything relates back to the core message and the core message provides purpose and context to all the secondary elements. The core message can be summed up in one sentence. It is the main thing that you want to get across, the main thing you want them to take away. Without clarity about the core message, very likely you will wander about and your listeners will become confused. But if all a good talk needed was a powerful core message, you could speak for 30 seconds and sit down!

II. Prayer

Pray to receive the message. Pray over all the elements in the message. Pray for the people you will be speaking to. Pray for the Lord to help you get your heart in just the right position: trusting Him and loving them. Pray for His anointing. Pray for Him to have His way. Then, release your cares to Him and step out in faith. When it comes to being prepared (in your head) for a talk or being pre-*prayer*-ed (in your heart), take prayer every time. Leave prayer out and the Lord may let you see just how well you can give a talk without Him! Depend too much on head knowledge and you will be "headed" for disaster.

III. Secondary Elements

Don't try to fit all of these secondary elements into your talk. That would be like trying to wear all of the clothes in your wardrobe in one day. Not every talk has to include all of these elements, but a good talk will include some of them. Pray and let the Lord lead you.

1) Scripture, Scripture, Scripture. Pick one or two key scriptures that illustrate your core message and seek to plant them deeply in their minds and hearts. This is what the Holy Spirit will most powerfully use to liberate them as they try to walk out the message they've heard. Scatter other scriptures generously about, but don't clutter the talk with them. Less is more when it comes to what people will remember in the take away.

2) Key Insights. Give credibility to what you are saying by adding insights from Christian leaders, or from facts you've gleaned from articles that are relevant.

3) Personal Testimony. There is no better way to illustrate or flesh out a teaching than with your own relevant experience. There are, however, some pernicious pitfalls to avoid. See below.

4) Humor. Bring in appropriate jokes or use your own. Remember that the joy of the Lord is our strength.[4] A spoonful of sugar helps the medicine go down, enabling us to take in the serious things He wants us to digest.

5) Ministry Times. Strike while the iron is hot! At the right time—as the Spirit prompts you—lead the group in confessional times of repentance and ministry. If the teaching is anointed, the hearts of your listeners will be touched. This creates tremendously fruitful opportunities to harvest their prayers or prune away their burdens. See below.

6) Quotations. Beware of long readings. Nowadays we seem to have little ability to stay focused on long readings or quotations. Unless it is very good and you can read it well, do some ruthless editing of your favorite material. Trim the fat; keep it lean and you will hold their attention.

7) Tone. To paraphrase Muhammad Ali the boxer, "float like a butterfly," but let the Lord "sting like a bee."[5] Our job is not to try to convict people, but to simply put the truth before them and let the Holy Spirit do it.

Testimony Guidelines

Personal testimony is powerful, but it is also dangerous—just like 220 volts of electricity. With your story used the right way you can electrify an audience. Use it the wrong way and you will electrocute them instead. Just because scripture says that we defeat the enemy "with the word of our testimony" doesn't mean that it works every time, regardless of how we use it.[6] Wisdom is required for the proper use of all of God's gifts, especially the most powerful ones. If you would rather leave your listeners exhilarated and alive, rather than bored to death, please follow these tips.

1) Never Overshadow the Truth. Don't let your experiences eclipse the real message. Personal experiences illustrate truth, they don't establish it. The truths you are teaching are what the Holy Spirit will use to help them in their time of trial, not your stories. Also, don't let the telling of your own story secretly capture your heart. That would become an inroad for pride. Let the truth your story is intended to illustrate be what your heart desires to express. That will lead you (and them) closer to Jesus, who is the Truth we are all seeking to live for.

2) Follow the 80/20 Principle: 80% teaching; 20% personal testimony. Think of truths as the meat and potatoes of the meal you are serving; personal testimonies are the gravy that makes truth taste great. Since no one can live on a diet of gravy, balance things out. As with any other art, once you become masterful at teaching you can safely bend and stretch the rules. No novice can. The 80/20 principle also applies to the operations of the two kingdoms. Keep a healthy balance between what the enemy did in your life to take you captive and what the Lord did to set you free—don't give the work of the enemy too much air time.

3) Keep It Short and Sweet. Although we tend to be forever fascinated by our own stories, the funny thing is, others aren't. Some select few can tell a long, winding personal story and not lose the interest of anyone in the room, but that's a *rare* gift. Best to be brief—cut to the chase!—and make sure everyone is with you. Don't be fooled. People will give you polite attention because it's your story and they don't want to hurt your feelings. That's not the same thing as an anointing!

4) Serve It Steaming H.O.T. Being Honest, Open and Transparent really draws out the anointing of the Spirit and draws in your listeners. We all love to catch privileged glimpses into the secrets of other lives—the HOT-er the better. This satisfies that inward hunger to know others more intimately. Many times the messenger becomes the message, showing us ways of living with God and people that we hardly dreamed possible. Just make sure that you aren't giving secrets away that will embarrass you later. There are things we don't need to know about each other and ways of sharing that can backfire, as the following three examples illustrate.

5) Beware of Glory Stories. For every two personal victory stories, be sure to tell at least one story of failure or of struggle with something that was hard for you to get. People can relate better to you if they see your common humanity. It gives them hope when they see that you are just like them: goofed up and having a hard time getting it. Beware of the subtle pride that wants to appear glorious in victory, even if you imagine you are giving glory to God.

6) Avoid Gory Stories. On the other hand don't share about areas of your life that are still raw and bleeding. Things that are too unhealed will cast a shadow over them, distracting them from truths you are teaching. Worse, you may speak from the darkness of your unhealed perspective instead of from His Light. Be careful not to use the class you are teaching as an occasion for personal therapy.

7) Resist Grousing Stories. Don't tell stories that put another person in a bad light—and you in a good light. This may be an unconscious way of getting revenge on people who have hurt you and also of making you a victim in the class's eyes. If you have to share something negative about someone, be sure you do it in a way that honors their dignity as a person. Don't encourage people to judge someone with you, or laugh at anyone in a way that diminishes them.

145

Ministry while Teaching

Sometimes the mood of the room will shift while you are teaching. Of course you can change the mood intentionally by reaching for humor or by quoting from something deathly serious. You can disrupt the mood accidentally by saying something confusing, or not quite true, or by straying off the mark. But suppose you are right on track and sense an anointing that is gracing what you are doing. Any unintended shift may be the Lord's way of calling you to lead the class through prayers that will help them process what you have just been teaching.

One obvious example of this would be a talk on forgiveness. If you suddenly sense you are losing them, it just may be that the Holy Spirit has them thinking about someone they need to forgive. They feel the tug of this and start remembering what happened. All you will feel is a sense that they are distracted by something. Just pause the lesson and ask if that's the case. If it is, ask them if it would be alright for you to lead them in a prayer to release forgiveness. Then walk them through it leaving nothing to chance. Most people need to be taught how to do these things. Model it for them or lead them word for word, however seems best.[7]

John Wimber, the founder of the Vineyard movement, would purposefully teach until the Holy Spirit began to fall on the people.[8] Then he would immediately stop teaching and begin praying for healing. Only the Lord knows how to mend broken hearts, dig up root issues, or bring closure to old wounds. We have to learn to watch for His timing. He looks into every heart far better than we can and knows when people are ready to surrender, trust and pray. Always ask permission to open an issue for confession and prayer. Then, follow the leading and let the Lord bring the message home!

---

[1] Romans 15:13: Truth is always liberating. Lies and half truths always put us into bondage. Every truth has a liberating potential. Watch how it works for you to give you "joy and peace" as you believe it. Then you will definitely want to share it with others: *May the God of hope fill you with all joy and peace in believing...*

[2] Phillips Brooks (1835-1893) was an Episcopal priest who is best known for writing "O Little Town of Bethlehem"—one of the few Christmas carols that explains the deeper meaning of the gospel. In his day his sermons and lectures drew capacity crowds. Brooks also introduced Helen Keller to Christianity as well as to Anne Sullivan. Sadly, I memorized these two quotations years ago, but lost track of where I found them.

[3] John 14:6: Falling in love with truth and falling in love with Jesus go hand in hand. Because Jesus is "the truth," getting passionate about one will always get you passionate about the other: *Jesus said to him, "I am the way, and the truth, and the life."*

[4] This well-known statement ironically came after the people had been brought to tears by hearing the Word of the Lord read to them. They were not to stay in that place of grief and conviction: Nehemiah 8:10: *This day is holy to our Lord. And do not be grieved, for the joy of the Lord is your strength.*

[5] Muhammad Ali (1942-) was a famous boxer during the 60s and 70s. As Cassius Clay he beat Sonny Liston for the heavyweight title in a stunning upset in 1964. You can see him speak this famous phrase on YouTube.

[6] The picture in Revelation 12:11 of power in testimony includes depth of character: *And they have conquered him [the enemy] by the blood of the Lamb and by the word of their testimony, for they loved not their lives even unto death.*

[7] What we call "The Lord's Prayer" was actually not His, but a prayer He taught the disciples. Don't assume people know how to pray. We all needed someone to show us the way, even if we don't remember the

moments of learning by listening when they happened for us: Luke 11:11: *Lord, teach us to pray, as John taught his disciples…*

[8] John Wimber (1934-1997) was a musician, pastor and a leader of the charismatic movement who founded the Vineyard movement. He did much to advance both the healing and the prophetic ministries of the Holy Spirit.

CHAPTER 15

PRAYER MINISTRY

This is only one of many ways of doing prayer ministry, but it has been highly effective. The great thing in the care of souls, as in medical practice, is to make sure you do more good than harm. This method—the ministry of The Keys— has led to many happy outcomes and it is frequently needed, for it deals with the common colds of the spiritual life. It has its limits, but it is a great, safe way of getting started.

"I will give you the keys of the kingdom of heaven, and whatever you bind on earth shall be bound in heaven, and whatever you loose on earth shall be loosed in heaven." Matthew 16:19

The Keys to Freedom

This is a ministry of the keys to freedom. It is primarily about helping people to get emotional and spiritual release and freedom from issues that they are already aware of struggling with. This is not about doing deliverance or going deeply into a person's inner depths. You can do a lot of damage that way. Stick to the three keys, especially in the beginning. They will bring a great deal of immediate relief and launch them into a healing journey that they will be able to maintain themselves. Know your limits: There are always some people you simply aren't equipped enough to minister to (yet). If you are serious about pursuing this, it would

149

be a good idea to take our free online eCourse for Healing just to make sure that you understand the ways the Lord heals us emotionally, and can recognize emotional strongholds and help people overcome them.

> **CAUTION:** If your church already has ministry teams, join them. These lessons may complement, confirm or enhance what you will be learning from them. The best way to learn ministry is always from people who are already doing it successfully. Do not, therefore, go off on your own, if the Lord has already set before you leaders who can teach you.[1] These chapters are solely for the purpose of giving elementary instruction to those of you who have no one reasonably nearby to learn from — and you honestly believe the Lord is calling you to get involved. In that case the best you can do is learn what you can by written word, pray and proceed with caution, walking humbly with your God.

The keys to freedom include but are not limited to these three: receiving forgiveness, releasing forgiveness, believing truth (the restoration promises of God).

1) Receiving Forgiveness. Just because a person has received faith in Jesus and has prayed for their sins to be forgiven, doesn't mean that they have fully benefited from the gift that they have received. Wherever there is guilt or shame, regret or self-blame, a fear of God's displeasure, or anxieties about their salvation, there is an obvious need for this key. It may have to be combined with the other keys, since any unforgiveness can easily block the grace needed to fully receive God's mercy.[2] Likewise, any unbelief regarding the promises of God concerning

His loving, gracious nature and His willingness and ability to bring restoration, also can block the effective use of this key.[3]

2) Releasing Forgiveness. This key is vital to our growth in the spiritual life. There can be no freedom or healing if a person holds on to bitter judgments against God, self or others. People often need a lot of coaching and some word for word leading to cross this hurdle once they have become ready. That we have to "fully forgive" everyone for anything is clearly stated in scripture and well-known, if too-seldom obeyed.[4] But we also must forgive ourselves just as fully and freely as God does.[5]

Ironically, once a person truly forgives and accepts themselves at a depth level (for the sinner that they are apart from Christ), then it becomes much easier for them to give the same mercy to others. Often missed is how we need to "forgive" God. The Lord never sins or makes a mistake, but in our heart of hearts we often blame Him for what He allows. This is technically, not forgiving God (He is innocent), but releasing Him from our own bitter judgments.

3) Believing Truth. All Christians are believers, but that doesn't mean that any of us are automatically and forever free of unbelief. Unbelief is a central component of discouragement, despair and depression. It inflames every fear and anxiety. It gives rise to every sinful attitude. If we believed the truths of God will a full heart of faith we would all be singing with the angels, no matter what has

151

happened to us or to our loved ones. It only takes a little unbelief to block a whole lot of faith. The primary truth we encourage everyone needing emotional healing to fully and absolutely believe is Romans 8:28: "We know all things work together for good for those who love God."

A Model Session

This model assumes that a good deal of instruction in basic issues of inner healing has come first, including the three keys. Without generous preparation much teaching will have to happen during the session. With sufficient prior teaching, the individual will come in far more willing and able to cooperate. Our model in the past provided up to 40 hours of group teaching sessions, many of which included group ministry sessions. A lot of healing and deliverance happened both during the lessons (as the lights went on) and during the group ministry times (as the issues were dealt with *en mass*). At the end of it all would come the individual ministry times, usually of only ½ to one hour in duration. It is easy to pull weeds (issues) after so much good rain!

Since the heart remains broken wherever hurt or loss is still felt in the memory, the person's sense of pain can be a reliable guide to where the break occurred. Only Jesus can heal the broken heart, but prayers of repentance and reconciliation are necessary for Him to be able to do His work. So, cast your cares on Him and get your heart ready, because the session is about to start.

I. Open

Introduce yourself and your prayer partner(s). Go over any directions or explanations that may be necessary to orient them and put them at ease. Pray to begin the session.

II. Explore

It is OK to start with where they are at present (the bad fruit they are dealing with), but always be looking for the roots (the issues that are lodged further back in the past). Part of the problem people have in getting free is too much focus on present problems and too little willingness to pull up and look at the painful issues that they have buried. We want to help them resolve some of those buried issues with the help of the three keys.

There are two questions to ask which will help them get focused.

1) Where are you stuck? What key issue(s) are you still struggling with?

2) Where does it still hurt?

If they are not sure, begin with their earliest relationships and earliest memories. Go over their relationship with father and mother, then other close family members as they were growing up. It saves time if you have had them fill out a brief confidential ministry form which you can review before the session.

Do not allow rambling on. Sometimes people start talking about a loved one's problems, or their own self-pity may divert and derail the real issues. Remind them, that this time is for them and their issues. You are not looking for everything, but for one or two crucial areas where their heart was broken. Once you have a sense of the source of their pain you are ready to begin prayers. You can't get to it all, nor do you need to. Stay focused.

III. Apply the Keys

Take the pain and apply the keys of the kingdom once you ask them if they are ready and willing to do the repenting that seems to be needed.

1. Receive. Repent of any sins (i.e. agreements with the enemy) and *receive* forgiveness.

2. Release. Repent of the sin of un-forgiveness towards God, self or others and *release* forgiveness.

3. Restore. Repent of any unbelief (especially in the promises of restoration), choose to *believe* God's truth as it applies, and be restored to trusting Him.

Most people will need you to lead them out loud and word for word in how to pray.[6] When the prayers are completed, rebuke any spirits you discern, and then pray for God to heal the broken heart.

Let the Holy Spirit convict—do not force recognition of a sin upon them. If they will not take steps to forgive, gently speak to them about the necessity of forgiveness and let them know that you cannot effectively minister beyond that point. Ask if they will at least pray "Lord, help me want to want to forgive them" as an invitation to God to begin working with their hearts.

What if the person refuses to repent? Here is a suggestion. Ask them: "In your ignorance, you sinned. In their ignorance, they sinned against you. Are you willing to forgive? If not, are you willing to confess that as sin?"

IV. Close

Ask Jesus to speak to them His words of comfort and guidance now and in the days ahead. Allow time for the Lord to speak. Ask what they have heard (if anything). It is not necessary that they hear a word from the Lord, but it is something to celebrate with them if they do. Many people are so wounded or poorly equipped that they don't know how to recognize the way the Lord speaks, so don't dwell on this if they can't.

Remind them to walk it out. The enemy is certain to come around tempting them to fall back into their former heart attitudes. They need to be on guard against this, resist him when it happens, and trust that the Lord will ultimately use such attacks to deepen their freedom.

Close with prayers of thanksgiving and infilling of the Spirit. Make sure they have come to at least a measure of peace and release before closing. Sometimes you cannot get a point of pain healed, but you can always pray for the Lord to close the wound and heal it in the future.

As you can see the ministry of inner healing is primarily a ministry of helping people discover where they need to repent and then helping them do it by the use of the three keys. What did we expect? Sin is unhealthy! It locks us out of the very place of freedom from pain and freedom for joy that we want to get into. That's why these kingdom keys are so effective: they enable us to "repent for the kingdom of God is at hand."[7] Jesus knew we would need them!

---

[1] That could be rebellion and pride. Let others *disciple* you and the Lord won't have to *discipline* you. That principle always sounded like wisdom to me.

[2] Mark 11:25: *Forgive… so that your Father also who is in heaven may forgive you your trespasses.*

[3] This promise could easily have us all shouting for joy in any situation— if we *fully* believed it with the faith we have already been given: Romans 8:28: *We know that for those who love God all things work together for good…*

[4] Matthew 18:32-35: *So also my heavenly Father will do to every one of you, if you do not forgive your brother from your heart.*

[5] This loving of self in the right way is included in the second of the two great commandments: Matthew 22:39-40: *You shall love your neighbor as yourself.*

[6] See "How to Forgive" in our Healing Articles at healingstreamsusa.org for 10 steps to lead people through in releasing forgiveness.

[7] Mark 1:14-15: *The kingdom of God is at hand; repent and believe in the gospel.*

CHAPTER 16

VALUES AND GUIDELINES

Thanks to the ministry of inner healing and deliverance, there are countless thousands, perhaps millions, of Christians who have been marvelously healed and set free. Sadly, there are also others who have been thrown deeper into bondage and pain, because the enemy was able to use over-zealous and under-trained ministers to cause damage. When the footing is potentially treacherous, it is always best to slow down, walk carefully and pray a lot. Let these values and guidelines give you balance and show the way to mend old wounds without causing new ones.

It was not because we do not have that right, but to give you in ourselves an example to imitate.
2 Thessalonians 3:9-10

A Good Example

We all benefit from a good example. Paul lived his beliefs out before the eyes of everyone in the churches he planted, intentionally giving them an example to imitate. Consider how this helped them. By Paul's teaching they knew (for instance) that Jesus had given them the Golden Rule to follow, but they never had the chance to see Jesus during His lifetime.[1] How should they apply it? In Paul himself these new converts could see that rule fleshed out in countless ways.

These are values and guidelines learned from the teaching and example of many leaders in the field of Christian ministry. For those of us who have been mentored by the direct example of a great leader, the image is impressed on one's heart. Such a person need only consider, "How would my mentor have handled this?" and the right thoughts spring instantly to mind. For the rest of us, learning by their stated values and guidelines will do just as well, if we take them to heart.

Go over these two lists slowly and prayerfully. Take time to really think them through. See how they would apply in your own life and ministry. Then thank God that you can learn from a good example and not have to find these things out for yourself the hard way.[2]

Values surrounding Ministry

1) Stay Connected. If you want to disciple others, you must be a disciple yourself. That means keeping the Big Five (Bible, prayer, worship, fellowship and service) in good working order in your life, so that you are doing your level best to trust Jesus, deny yourself, and follow Him daily.[3]

2) Live Cleansed. If you want God to use you to help others get free of sin, you have to be dedicated to repenting of and resisting sin in your own life as the Holy Spirit shows you. No compromise!

3) Keep Healing. If you want God to use you to bring emotional healing to others, you have to let Him into all of your wounds. You don't have to be fully healed (or none of us could have started), but you should be more healed than wounded (otherwise your wounds will get in the way).

4) Walk in Love. Maintaining good relationships is essential to ministry and to life. Keep short accounts with others. Do all in your power to be at peace with them.[4]

5) Be Submitted. Mutual love includes respect and submission, intimacy and accountability.[5] This means being connected to the Body of Christ in some meaningful way through a church or a home fellowship and allowing those relationships to test and grow you.

6) Release Others. Agape love allows the other person to be free to be themselves. No one likes being badgered by a controlling person, a fault finder or a busy body—for good reason: "Where the Spirit of the Lord is there is liberty."[6]

7) Avoid All Judging. Never mistake the shadow side for the person who cast it. Try to see everyone as a new creation deep down (if they are Christians) or in potential (if they are unbelievers).[7] Practice separating people from their sins in the way you see them—just as Jesus does.

8) Cover Others. Confidentiality acts as a covering to one another and guards each one's dignity. Wounded people are sensitive to any words that expose their nakedness.[8] Whenever the Lord allows you to see their vulnerability, pain or shame, it is a sacred trust. Never violate it.

9) No Gossip! Speak about others only in a way you wouldn't mind being overheard by them. This eliminates both spreading gossip and sowing division.[9]

10) Avoid Accusations. Don't go around saying "so and so has a spirit of ___." Who does that help? That's just your guess. You don't know that as a fact unless God has given you vision into the invisible realm and if He has, save it for a time of ministry. Otherwise, you would be doing the work of "the Accuser of the brethren" for him.[10]

11) Respect the Bride. Don't speak ill of Christian leaders, churches, or denominations. Honor His Bride. Always remember that Jesus loves His church and that the church is first and foremost His people, but it also includes those institutional bodies He has been working with for two millennia. If the organized church looks like a mess to you, what does that tell you about how you view His leadership over it?[11]

12) Persevere with Patience. Speaking the truth in love, revealing the hurt of our heart, releasing forgiveness and entering into God's rest (by believing a promise of His over the situation that concerns you) really do usher in God's way of bringing change. Be patient, keep the faith, stay within these boundaries and you will see genuine transformations happen by the Hand of the Lord.

13) Silence Is Golden. Only friendship and leadership convey the privilege of giving words of correction. Don't presume that you have a right to tell others what you think about them or their behavior. Just think how many people Jesus could have spoken to about their sins, but didn't. (The answer is everyone He met.)

14) Try to Relax. No one has to be perfect, just willing to try to stay within the proper boundaries while they are growing. Perfection is our unachievable goal.[12] We will never be perfect this side of heaven, but we are dedicated to seeking it, because we are dedicated to seeking Him. We want to be as close to Him as possible and as like Him as possible. That's our burning desire!

15) Seek Honesty. There is plenty of room for failure, trial and error, and issues undergoing repair. Be honest, open and transparent and you will always find grace.[13] Mercy and love "cover a multitude of sins," but not a single excuse.[14]

16) Seek Humility. A teachable attitude, a yielded heart, a surrendered spirit are greatly to be prized. With them we will find grace to keep learning and growing.[15] Without them we may fall by the wayside and not even know it.

Guidelines during Ministry[16]

1) Minister in pairs with one in the lead. Jesus sent the disciples two by two.[17] Paul always took someone along on his missionary journeys. Married couples can be especially effective as a ministering team. Having a partner provides balance, the strength of mutual encouragement, and additional insight.

2) Avoid one-on-one ministry with a person of the opposite sex. We would prefer that ministry be men with men and women with women and seldom if ever be only men ministering to a woman or only women ministering to a man. If it needs to happen, see that you find a place where others are around. Watch out for unwise patterns developing in your behavior! Any secret desire to minister to someone of the opposite sex should be taken as a warning sign that the enemy is toying with your heart.

3) We minister the gospel—we do not give counsel, advice and direction, or make decisions for others. That is the Holy Spirit's job. Consider this: You can't even give consistently good advice and direction to yourself without the Holy Spirit helping you. We certainly can't take His place in other lives, no matter how tempting it seems.

4) We point to the scriptures that seem to speak to the situation, give encouragement, share our testimonies, offer our observations, suggest things to

consider, pray issues through, bless and love, bless and love.

5) If anyone—team member or attendee—receives a prophetic revelation, let it be brought to the leadership in private to be judged by them whether it is to be shared with others.

6) Be careful how and where you touch people as you minister to them. Some wounded people draw back at even the slightest touch. Always ask permission first, before laying on hands in prayer. Be aware that when praying for the opposite sex hands should not be placed lower than the shoulders. Ask a prayer partner of the same sex as the prayee to be the one to give an embrace, if it seems to be needed for the sake of ministry and would be welcomed.

7) We pray with our eyes open so that we can observe what is going on with the person who is being ministered to. You will want to see how the Lord is moving upon them, or if the enemy is manifesting. Encourage them to simply relax, receive and focus on the Lord. If they begin praying in tongues, gently ask them to remain quiet instead.

8) We do not speak in tongues out loud. People are coming to meet the Healer, not the Baptizer. If you feel led to pray in tongues, do so quietly within yourself.

9) We do not do guided visualizations or tell Jesus what to do in anyone's memory.

10) We never try to recover lost memories. That is something no one can rightly interpret or judge, since none of us were there. The Lord says that only He can search out the hidden mysteries of the heart—don't presume that you can. Many people have been unjustly slandered by this practice. Ordinary remembrances during ministry don't bring sweeping reversals of life events. Such memories you can work with. Beyond this you are getting in over your head. Have the good sense to admit your ignorance and close with prayer.

11) Don't diagnose their physical or psychological problems. You are not their doctor or psychiatrist. Don't undermine their relationship with theirs.

12) We never tell the person to stop taking medicines or medical treatment. If they have truly been healed, their doctor will want to get them off the medicine.

13) We do not pronounce the person healed or guarantee that they will be healed, no matter how strongly we may believe that it is coming. We hold out hope and encourage their hope. Let the Lord prove His work in His time.

14) Draw the person into recognition for themselves concerning the area you see as the potential blockage or bondage which needs ministry. Remind them of teachings they have received during teaching time,

but do not accuse them of "having a spirit of _____." Ask the person if it would be OK to deal with or to pray for such and such. See if they have a witness of their own, before beginning.

15) Be sensitive and gentle. Don't pressure people to repent. Each person has to be ready to acknowledge and confess by their own recognition of sin as the Spirit turns on the lights within them. Some just won't be able to see it, but give them the benefit of the doubt. They are here because they want to be free. Let's not hold their blindness against them.

16) Do not allow your own emotional hurts to become part of ministry by going into your entire story. Using the good that came out of your testimony may be helpful, but be brief and to the point. Keep the focus on the person you are ministering to, not yourself.

17) Don't show your insecurities. We all receive better if the person doing ministry with us is confident, peaceful and at rest. Remind yourself that you are only the vessel—Jesus is the true Healer present and to Him belongs the glory. It's not about you and what you can do. It's about Him and what He *may* do through you. Let your sense of inadequacy draw you into trust and dependence on Him.

18) Don't be legalistic—God isn't. Flow with the Spirit. The Lord will leave out some things you thought necessary and bring in other things you

wouldn't have imagined, if you let Him stay in the lead. Jesus sees the hearts of all involved. He is working even when we don't feel it or see it. Sometimes the best thing to come out of a session isn't something anyone noticed at the time.

19) Relax. Know that the person's healing and progress in the Lord does not depend upon you. Let the weight of the concern for the ministry time truly fall on Him. You are not their only hope—Jesus is. Even if the ministry time doesn't go as well you hoped or as far as you desired, remember that Jesus will still be with them. Pray every sense of lack or failure back into to His Hands.

20) Honor the confidentiality of what you see or hear. Carefully guard their identities and issues. Beware of wanting to boast about a good session later and you won't fall so low when the not so good ones happen!

Now that's a lot of things to remember! If you focus too much on specific rules you'll run the risk of being tripped up by guidelines, rather than helped by them. Genuine Christianity isn't about rule keeping anyway. It's about trusting and following the One who created the rules and who Himself keeps all of them by an effortless grace. If we yield ourselves to His leadership, His Spirit will lift and lead us into doing the right thing at the right time. Besides, it's well known that Jesus simplified all of the rules into one: Do unto others as you would have them do unto you. The Golden Rule is the rule of spiritual friendship. With every person we meet in ministry, we are being given an opportunity to make a friend for all eternity. Such friendship is our highest value, because it is also His.

> **No longer do I call you servants, for the servant does not know what his master is doing; but I have called you friends, for all that I have heard from my Father I have made known to you. You did not choose me, but I chose you and appointed you that you should go and bear fruit and that your fruit should abide, so that whatever you ask the Father in my name, he may give it to you. These things I command you, so that you will love one another.** John 15:15-17

Seen in this light the Golden Rule positively shines through all the values and guidelines of this chapter. We give them to you as a way of fleshing out that prime directive with specific applications. As you read through them, your heart agreement with them actually gives the Holy Spirit permission to bring them to your remembrance as situations arise. Those little nudges, if we are being attentive, are what keep the ministry on track—one further example of why we can't do Christian ministry without the Holy Spirit helping us. Fortunately, we don't have to. He is always right there inside of us, ready to power us up from within and right there above us, ready to bring heaven down when we call. May your adventure in ministry be one of growing an ever-greater love for God the Father, Jesus, the Holy Spirit and that sea of lost, hurting humanity surrounding you.

You have been chosen.
Now, go and bear much fruit!

---

[1] The "Golden Rule" is given by Jesus in Matthew 7:12: *So whatever you wish that others would do to you, do also to them, for this is the Law and the Prophets.*

[2] My Dad loved to say, "Experience is a hard school, but a fool will learn in no other." He was right—I should have paid more attention…

[3] Luke 9:23-24: *Let him deny himself and take up his cross daily and follow me.*

[4] Romans 12:18: *If possible, so far as it depends on you, live peaceably with all.*

[5] Titus 3:1-2: *Remind them to be submissive to rulers and authorities… and to show perfect courtesy toward all people.*

[6] 2 Corinthians 3:17 KJV: *And where the Spirit of the Lord is, there is liberty.*

[7] 2 Corinthians 5:17 *Therefore, if anyone is in Christ, he is a new creation…*

[8] Genesis 9:20-25 shows how others feel about having their "nakedness" exposed, even if it was by their own sin that they were made vulnerable to prying eyes.

[9] 2 Corinthians 12:20: *There may be quarreling, jealousy, anger, hostility, slander, gossip.*

[10] Revelation 12:10 KJV: *For the accuser of our brethren is cast down.*

[11] When scripture says Jesus is the Head this is not a mere title of respect, but a description (at the very least) of all that a head means to *any* body: Colossians 1:18: *And he is the head of the body, the church.*

[12] This command of Jesus finds balance and expression in the life and words of Paul. First Jesus: Matthew 5:48: *You therefore must be perfect*; Then, Paul: Philippians 3:12: *Not that I have already obtained this or am already perfect, but I press on to make it my own.*

[13] Isaiah 57:15: *I dwell in the high and holy place, and also with him who is of a contrite and lowly spirit, to revive the spirit of the lowly, and to revive the heart of the contrite.*

[14] 1 Peter 4:8: *Keep loving one another earnestly, since love covers a multitude of sins.*

[15] Let this prayer of David's become your daily desire: Psalms 51:10-12: *Renew a right spirit within me… and uphold me with a willing spirit.*

[16] Ephesians 5:15-17: *Therefore do not be foolish, but understand what the will of the Lord is*; 1 Peter 5:8: *Be sober-minded; be watchful. Your adversary the devil prowls around like a roaring lion, seeking someone to devour.*

[17] Mark 6:7: *And he called the twelve and began to send them out two by two…*

Appendix

*To our God and Father
be glory forever and ever. Amen.
The grace of the Lord Jesus Christ
be with your spirit.*
Philippians 4:20, 23

FORERUNNER MINISTRIES

Which hope we have as an anchor of the soul,
both sure and steadfast,
and which enters into that within the veil,
where the Forerunner has entered for us, even Jesus.
Hebrews 6: 19-20a MKJV

THE eCOURSE FOR HEALING
www.HealingStreamsusa.org

Practically everyone needs recovery of their heart from some painful issues of the past or could readily benefit from gaining mastery over their emotional turbulence in the present. The peace of Christ is meant to be a river of life that we experience all day long—no matter what our circumstances may be. Let the 24 main healing lessons and workout sessions of our free eCourse for Healing take your heart on pilgrimage to a place called the Kingdom of God that is already right inside you.

SPIRIT FILLED LIVING IN CHRIST
www.Forerunners4Him.org

Whether you are a brand new recruit or a "seasoned veteran," if you find that your peace levels are slipping and your joy is not full, then everything on this site is designed to help you come into the fullness of what it truly means to be saved by grace through faith—in all of your days and all of your situations. For us a forerunner is anyone who receives salvation and begins a lifetime quest of "running" into the Heart of God for intimacy and "going before the Lord" to prepare His way into other lives. That's your heart too, isn't it? Come get the equipping you need to be a liberated lover of Jesus and a loving liberator of others.

SANE AND SENSIBLE PERSPECTIVES
www.TheLastDays.info

Many people these days have a God-given hunger to know more about the Last Days. You'll find a feast at this website! Savor the taste of these "sane and sensible perspectives" which are salted with humor and spiced with fresh insights. We have extensive sections devoted to Signs of His Coming, When Is the Rapture, Crucial Components, and Ways to Prepare along with free downloads, an Updates section and blog. Best of all, an entire six-hundred-page commentary on The Book of Revelation is available for free reading and chapter by chapter download.

BOOKS FROM FORERUNNER

If you enjoyed this book, you can purchase copies for friends and keep exploring the spiritual life through these other insightful books by Steve Evans, available in paperback and eBook at Amazon.com.

The Book of Revelation takes you on a verse-by-verse stroll through the most complex prophetic vision ever given. These "sane and sensible perspectives" are guaranteed to help you see what this amazing book is trying to show us. With this detailed overview, you'll have the insights you'll need for the days to come.
624 pages. Paperback: $22.00. Kindle: $3.99.

Matters of the Heart is a 24 lesson workbook designed to guide Christian believers through the basic understandings necessary for releasing emotional damage from the past and gaining a grace-based restoration to wholeness. Each chapter is filled with "tools" for practical application.
278 pages. Paperback: $20.00.

The Missing Peace includes all of the 24 lessons of the *Matters of the Heart* teaching series, but without the workbook's other material, focusing instead on a stream of scriptural revelation that will show you how to bring your heart to God and receive His Heart for you in return.

194 pages. Paperback: $15.00.

Rescued from Hell chronicles one man's journey into a ten year living nightmare and his astonishing true story of return. Was it an insane delusion or a satanic deception? This is a tale both incredible and terrible, yet studded with life affirming humor and hope-filled insights into the spiritual realities that surround us.

190 pages. Paperback: $12.50.

An Illustrated Guide to the Spiritual Life captures in living color with playful insights the otherwise elusive, invisible realities of our life in God. This "illustrated devotional" includes explanations, scriptures and prayers. It is written for the general reader, but is also a pictorial companion to *The Missing Peace*.

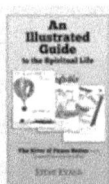

126 pages. Paperback: $17.50.
The River of Peace Series, Vol. 1.

Good Grief is not for everyone, but for those who despite their pain have "set their hearts on pilgrimage", determined to make it to the other side of the Valley of Tears, allowing sorrow that is *rightly* carried to mend their hearts and guide their lives toward God's new beginning.

70 pages. Paperback: $10.00.
The River of Peace Series, Vol. 2.

Salvation Basics provides easy to understand answers to life's most important questions: "What will happen to me when I die?" and "What can I do about it?" You will not only discover God's grace-filled way for getting you to heaven, but also His "secret" for living the heavenly life down here.

118 pages. Paperback: $10.00.
The River of Peace Series, Vol. 3.

Ministry Basics will prepare you to launch into the sea of human need, lostness and misery which surrounds you, finding your place in the Rescue and your highest path of purpose at the Lord's side. Let these field-tested truths equip you for a joy-filled lifetime of Holy Spirit empowered ministry.

163 pages. Paperback: $10.00.
The River of Peace Series, Vol. 4.

Knowing God may surprise you. The invisible God can be truly, intimately and delightfully known. But it gets even better because there are not just One of Him to get to know, but Three. Think of this as a guide book, not an encyclopedia. Three amazing Persons already know you and love you. What are you waiting for?

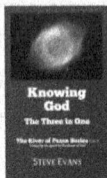

161 pages. Paperback: $10.00.

The River of Peace Series, Vol. 5.

Knowing Jesus will introduce you to the God-Man. He is far and away the most wonderful Person in the universe to know. And He can be known! Simply opening one's heart to Him is all He needs for that life-long adventure to begin. Let this "Spiritual Biography" lead you into fresh revelations of key moments in His life.

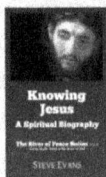

159 pages. Paperback: $10.00.

The River of Peace Series, Vol. 6.

Knowing the Spirit will introduce you to the Mystery Person of the Trinity, help you recognize His ways and connect with His presence, so that you can live with greater delight in His guidance and power. Let this book give you eyes to see and ears to hear your inner Guest as He works with you each day.

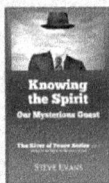

149 pages. Paperback: $10.00.

The River of Peace Series, Vol. 7.

Holy Spirit explores practical ways of getting to know the One who supplies us with supernatural power for life and ministry. Why should the Person of the Trinity who lives within us be so mysterious to us? This book combines *Knowing the Spirit* with *Ministry Basics* in a single, sensational volume.
171 pages. Paperback: $15.00.

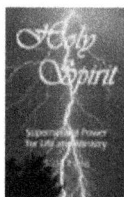

Jesus: An Intimate Portrait will give you fresh perspectives on His Story—the heroic story of the One who shapes all human history by His life and Word. Let these intimate insights reveal the living, breathing God-Man in ways you never encountered Him before. Seeing Him changes everything!
212 pages. Paperback: $15.00.

ABOUT THE AUTHOR

Steve Evans came to faith as one brought back from the dead after a decade of occult oppression and torment. His passion is to see people everywhere released from past brokenness and fully equipped for life and ministry. At HealingStreamsUSA.org he teaches believers how to recover their emotional freedom and master their inward state. At Forerunners4Him.org he shows how to live in the presence and power of the Spirit. His newest website, TheLastDays.info, gives "sane and sensible perspectives" on the events of the Last Days that are heading our way.

Steve has authored numerous books, including: *The Missing Peace, The Book of Revelation, Salvation Basics, Ministry Basics, Knowing the Spirit* and *Rescued from Hell* which tells the story of his own harrowing descent into inner darkness and ultimate restoration. Steve is an ordained minister and a former carpenter, craftsman and missionary.